Bums
on Seats

Bums on Seats

HOW TO PUBLICISE YOUR SHOW

HELEN SHARMAN

A & C Black · London

First published 1992
A & C Black (Publishers) Limited
35 Bedford Row, London WC1R 4JH

ISBN 0–7136–3662–9

A CIP catalogue record for this book is available from the British Library.

Cover illustration by Linda Costello.

Typeset by Florencetype Ltd, Kewstoke, Avon
Printed in Great Britain by Biddles Ltd,
Guildford, Surrey

Contents

Acknowledgements

My thanks go to Clare Murrell for preparing the poster designs and to Norman Robson for the photographs.

I would also like to thank all the members of Beaconsfield Theatre Group, for their advice and support.

Introduction: Curtain up

Theatre cannot exist without an audience. An obvious statement, but the audience is often the last thing in the mind of a group planning a performance and up to the neck in set-building and rehearsals. Much arm-twisting goes on to find a director and stage manager, time and care are spent selecting actors, a little gentle persuasion will find prompter and props, but a publicity secretary is often at the bottom of the list. This is where you come in . . .

Show and tell

Whatever your performance – musical, drama, open air, festival – the main reason for all the effort that goes into it is to give pleasure and to enjoy yourselves by entertaining an audience.

Good publicity can make or break a theatre group

It is heart-breaking for a team that has spent several months, not to mention all the blood, sweat and tears, to put on a first-rate production in front of a mere handful of friends and relatives.

More serious, a group that does not pay its way cannot afford to put on that delightful costume drama, that spectacular musical, or improve the lighting and may even be forced to shut down altogether.

Be proud of your show and make sure that the world, or at least your local area, knows all about it.

This book is intended as a guide through the maze of the publicity world. The ideas are presented as a starting point for planning and executing a campaign that is right for your particular group. All performing groups are different in terms of membership, venue, budget and so on, but share the common goal of the elusive 'House Full' notice.

Go fishing

Catching an audience is like catching a fish – a mixture of planning, patience and good luck. Choose your bait, cast your line, hook your target, then reel it in and, most important, hang on to it – audiences like fish, are slippery customers.

Good luck – and good fishing!

1
Setting up the publicity machine

Publicity is about advertising and selling. To sell anything success-fully, the product – in your case a theatre group – must have a clear identity, an image that is easily remembered. Think of yourselves as a packet of cornflakes, or a washing powder. You recognize your favourite brand a mile off, you buy it because you like it and, if this time it has a free plastic widget for the kids, or a money-saving offer for you, then that is a bonus.

It is the same with theatre. Play your cards right, and people will come simply because it is your group – they've been before and they like what they have seen. A well-known thriller or a romping farce is your free gift. A box-office play or musical is a bonus to your regulars, and an attraction to others to come for the first time.

A word of warning – all the publicity in the world will not turn a third-rate show into a smash hit. Your colleagues in the spotlight have to keep their end of the bargain. Deliver the goods and entertain your audience, they will be back. Bore the pants off them or embar-rass them and you won't see them for dust!

The publicity machine

Good publicity does not happen by accident. It takes thought and planning, time and money.

Why publicity?

Too many groups take a very cavalier attitude to publicity. They leave it until the last minute, when it is far too late to have any significant impact on ticket sales, and then complain that the posters have been a waste of money, and the press never come anyway. There will be those who have the mistaken belief that an audience will somehow magically appear as the curtain rises. It won't.

Ticket sales not doing too well? – not to worry it will be all right on the night. It won't be.

3

The company is short of cash – what can we save on publicity? Less publicity = smaller audience = less money.

Those who have never done the job often consider publicity as a pushover. Order a few posters, type a programme and give the press a quick ring the week of the show – nothing to it. Show them this book.

Effective publicity needs organization. The key is to have a system that will make sure something happens. Publicity must be somebody's special responsibility, and not farmed out to whoever happens to drift into rehearsal the week before the show. The first task is to design a publicity machine that suits your particular group and that harnesses the manpower you have available.

Solo or chorus?

The size of a group gives a strong indication of how much publicity work it will realistically be able to handle. The size of the group's bank balance will indicate how much it can afford.

A band of less than twenty enthusiastic members will probably be unable to spare more than one of their number for this job. If this is the case, then the amount of publicity angles should be restricted. Unless you have a super-efficient person, it is not reasonable to expect him or her to organize posters, tickets, call the press and arrange a complicated sponsorship deal all at the same time.

A bigger group may well be able to form a small publicity sub-committee, and divide the work. For example, one person can handle posters, handbills and tickets, another can be appointed press officer, and so on.

Whatever the choice your group makes, ensure that no individual is overloaded. Given too many tasks, the poor soul will end up with sleepless nights and nightmares about missed deadlines. He, or she, may refuse to do the job ever again and, since continuity is a major advantage in publicity, the group will lose out.

It is worthwhile appointing a publicity secretary for a season rather than for a single event. Assistants can come and go, but it will save both time and effort if one person has done it before. The job is made easier if there is a good relationship with the press, a knowledge of local contacts – and the quirks of your printer. At the very least, the publicity secretary should be encouraged to build up a detailed job description, together with a folder of phone numbers and helpful hints that can be passed to a successor. The relevant details should be up-dated on a regular basis. This folder also means that should your key publicity person fall ill, or be out of the country, it is easier for someone else to step into the breach.

Survival kit

A publicity secretary, either solo, or as part of the team, needs few basic qualifications, and little equipment to do a good job.

- A telephone – *absolutely essential*.
- A typewriter or word-processor.
- The local telephone and yellow-pages directories.
- A diary and notebook *always* next to the phone.

Local knowledge is an asset

Knowledge of the group is also a terrific advantage. However good newcomers may be, it is unfair to throw them into the job until they have been around the group, and the area, for at least a year.

Finally, an ideal publicity person has an enquiring and creative mind, is organized and has the ability to work effectively on the telephone.

The name game

If your company is new, and nameless, you have *carte blanche* in what you call it – well almost.

Go for a connection.

> **Place** Incorporate the name of the town, of the theatre or venue where you perform, or of the street where it stands. No permanent home? Then make that work for you – what about 'The Gypsy Theatre Company'?

> **Organization** If the members are drawn from a particular. company, profession, school or college, use the common bond as a basis for the name. Be creative, for example, a group of engineers could call themselves 'The Nuts and Bolts Players'.

> **Membership** All women group? Over-sixties? Under-twenty-ones? – there could be names there.

> **Type of production** Your group may be formed specifically to put on Shakespeare, or experimental theatre, musicals or only comedy – use this in your title and make the public aware of what you are selling. Think of the professional names – 'The Royal National Opera Company' or 'The Theatre of Comedy', for example.

> **Image** A name that conjures up attractive associations can also work well. 'The Masque Players', 'The Minstrels', have direct

links with drama and music, but more abstract names have their place too – 'Questors' Theatre', 'Four Square Players', for example.

Avoid confusion

Having spent a happy evening in the pub dreaming up your new name, always go back in the cold light of day and check that you are not treading on anybody else's toes. Calling yourselves 'The Masque Players', with another group called 'The Masqueraders', two miles up the road, will not please them, and will confuse your audience.

It is worth ensuring that you do not conflict with any local businesses or major products. Manufacturers and companies go to great lengths to protect the names that they trade under and the majority of product names are registered. So be careful. If you even half suspect that there could be a clash, contact your potential 'rival' direct, and ask. A letter is cheaper than a court case.

More than likely, you will find a combination of all these ideas is the one for you, but beware of initials. A long name is frequently reduced to first letters, so the St Oswaldtwistle Dramatic Society can end up with an entirely different image from the one that was intended!

Logo

A logo is quite simply the trademark of a group. It can be anything from a coat of arms to a design made up of initials, or a pictograph, for example, the classic, though somewhat overworked, image of two masks of comedy and tragedy. This visual shorthand can be invaluable in pushing a performing group into the minds of the public. Go for a bold symbol and avoid too much detail. That brilliant line drawing of your theatre will become a blur to anyone more than a few feet away.

The temptation to go overboard with the use of colour should be strongly resisted – colour printing is expensive – don't go using a rainbow as your symbol! If you feel a touch of colour would enhance your design, fine, but only use one, and ensure that the design will still work if reproduced in black and white.

You may have a graphic designer in your midst who would be only too delighted to come up with a few ideas. If not, don't panic, sketch out a rough design, then seek out a professional to turn it into finished artwork. Artwork is expensive, but the investment is worthwhile, as your logo can be put to a whole variety of uses.

> ***Publicity material*** Handbills, posters, banners, programmes, car stickers.

Letter heading Ideal for the secretary when booking rehearsal rooms, writing to sponsors, confirming orders, etc. It can even be used as an emergency receipt.

Group 'uniform' Sweat shirts, T-shirts, badges, etc.

Don't let the idea of a 'uniform' put you off. It is not compulsory!

Badges or sweat shirts can really work for a group. Wear them on a publicity drive in your town, wear them when you are working on the set – and in the pub afterwards! It's a great way to start a conversation and get yourselves noticed.

These items should be self-funding and can even make a small profit. Look in the local yellow pages, the local paper, or a publication like *Marketing Week* to find suppliers. Then collect a few estimates. At today's prices a sweat shirt will come out at around £10–15, badges for as little as 10p. Add a bit extra and sell them to your members, Hey presto! – a few more pennies in the group's coffers.

My own group has found sweat shirts far more successful than T-shirts, mainly because most of our activity takes place in the winter months. Even in the summer, have you noticed how it always rains when you try to paint scenery in the car park!

Baiting the hook

Right, you have a group, you have a venue, all you need now is an audience . . . and a play.

Remember: however good your publicity, the show itself has a significant effect on your box office. You will have your 'regulars' – those who will turn up to almost anything you do, from Chekhov to farce, Wagner to Gilbert and Sullivan, but if you are aiming for those elusive 'House Full' notices, you need to catch the floating voters.

Comedies and thrillers always go down well, but don't bore your members by doing nothing else. Be prepared to take risks and include plays that *you* want. Restoration comedy and Chekhov do not have mass appeal, but they provide a challenge for the actors, and demonstrate that the group has versatility and variety. The same goes for musical societies – Gilbert and Sullivan will pull in the crowds, *Tannhäuser* may have a less instant response. Sprinkle these 'minority' items into your programme when your budget allows and aim to break even rather than make a huge profit.

Musicals and orchestral concerts have a head start in numbers and ticket sales, but they also demand excellent audience figures to cover the heavy costs of this type of full-blown production. There is no denying that a big cast sells more tickets than a two-hander. It is much easier to persuade people to come to see someone they know than to get them along to watch a cast of complete unknowns. Unfortunately any non-professional performance often gets pigeon-holed with school concerts – people go out of loyalty to individuals, with no expectation of enjoying themselves. The standard of the performance is in the hands of the director and cast, but it is up to you, the publicity person, to ensure that the public do not miss out on a high-quality production.

Work hard to get the public on your seats, give them a good night out, entertain them, and with a bit of luck you will convert them into regulars.

Balance the season

The right play or musical at the right time can make a difference to your box office and to the financial health of a group. Seek your treasurer's advice. Get hold of a copy of his records for the last five years or so, and take a long hard look. Is there a seasonal pattern to your audience figures? Many groups find that they sell more tickets for a November production than for a May show. To provide a balance, November can be scheduled for productions that are heavy on costume and set, and May can take a low-budget show.

A musical society usually has a different set of financial parameters. The costs of hiring orchestra, sets and costumes are so high that often they find the group can support only one major production a year. Again, look at the best time to do it, then ask whether the group could do a second, less ambitious, show in the year, for example, a cabaret, a selection of songs from famous musicals, an Andrew Lloyd Webber evening, a programme of Noël Coward. This approach keeps the group active and motivated, keeps the society in front of the public, and, one hopes, may even make some money to support the next major undertaking.

If your group is in the habit of doing a show in December/January, then this is the ideal time to attract families. Go for a pantomime, or something similar that will play to a packed matinee of little ones – crisp packets and all – *Toad of Toad Hall* rather than *Waltz of the Toreadors*.

Look at your rivals

Keep a close eye on what other companies in your area are doing, both amateur and professional. There is a strange telepathic link between theatrical groups and sudden explosions of Agatha Christie or Oscar Wilde are more common than you might think! Five pro-ductions of *The Importance of Being Earnest* in a ten-mile radius within four weeks of each other will *all* lose out.

Try to get your name onto the mailing lists of local venues and societies.

8

Order a copy of *Amateur Stage*. This monthly publication carries listings of amateur societies, both operatic and dramatic, for the next two months. Even better, make a personal contact with your equivalent in other local groups and ask what their plans are. It should not be a trade secret and it is as much in their interest as yours.

Order a regular copy of *The Stage*, the professional weekly paper, and check what is touring in your locality. The publishers of the play may be happy to release the copyright, but it is still possible to clash with a professional company touring the same play.

2
Posters, handbills and leaflets

No matter how good your material, or your performers, you will play to only a handful of faithful friends and relatives if nobody else knows about it.

The style of publicity that you adopt, and the precise package that you use, will vary from group to group. As a guideline, the main tools of your trade are as follows:

- Posters.
- Handbills/leaflets.
- Local press.
- Banners and sign boards.
- Local radio.
- Mailing list.

Posters

A good poster should grab attention. Work with the producer, to come up with a design idea that conveys something of the style of the play.

A word of caution – make sure that clear lines of responsibility are established, as to who has the final say on the design. Ideally, in all matters, except the basic image of the performance itself, the decision should lie with publicity, not the producer. He or she has only one show on his or her mind, you have the whole season and the overall identity of the group.

An over-enthusiastic director can wreck a carefully built-up image by deciding that your now established logo is out of keeping with his concept of the specific production. On the other hand, a fresh approach can be valuable, so *always* listen.

Obviously a poster should carry the essential details, what, where, when, and how to get tickets, but to make it really work for you, it must have impact.

Poster design is a complex juggling act with the elements of impact, image and information.

With any luck you will have an artistic individual in your group, or someone will know someone who can provide the necessary artwork. Your printer may be able to help. A printing company that specializes in theatrical posters, such as Cowdalls in Crewe, keeps a stock of illustrations which are available for a reasonable fee (see Appendix: Useful addresses).

Keep the design simple. Avoid too much detail and include a good measure of black which will stand out.

Colour

The colour scheme of a poster is the first thing that catches the eye of the casual observer. Obviously, the designer will have a major say in the final choice, but here are a few tips.

Strangely enough, theatre posters are fashion conscious in their choice of colours. Take a look at a current poster from the National Theatre or the RSC for an indication of this year's tints. Think carefully about the background colour. A bright Day-glo poster will make its presence felt among the jumble sale notices in a newsagent's window, but may be totally out of keeping with the production.

Be creative. Brown on cream can be distinctive, and give an authentic feel to a poster for Old Time Music Hall, or melodrama.

A design that requires more than one colour ink may look terrific, but is more expensive. Why not try the DIY approach and use a felt tip pen! My own group produced a dramatic poster for *Deathtrap* by this method. The basic design was a black crossbow on a white background, with the drops of bright red blood coloured in later.

Black on white may convey all the relevant information, but without a well-thought-out design, this style of poster can become nothing more than camouflage for a shop window. Pastel backgrounds can have the same problem.

Look at the two photographs on pages 12–13 of Wotnot Theatre Group's poster for *The Storm*. First, the image itself.

Poster 2 certainly has an interesting design, but little or no impact. The frame round the lightning helps, but it gives the impression of an ordnance-survey map. The thin black lines stop abruptly and the eye is led off to the left and, consequently, to whatever else may be next to it. Black and white should be handled with care and this poster is a classic candidate for camouflage.

Poster 1, on the other hand, will get itself noticed. Not only is the solid black of the background dramatic and eye-catching, but the

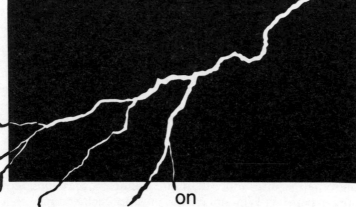

WOTNOT THEATRE GROUP
PRESENT

THE STORM

BY WILLIAM BREAKSPEARE

on
14th, 15th & 16th April 1992
at
The Church Hall, Fenton

Starting at –   Tickets –
Evening 8.00pm   Adults   £2.50
Sat Mat 3.00pm   Children/OAPs £1.50

BOX OFFICE – FENTON 0321 3286

1. A successful poster: a dramatic design that attracts attention, with all the essential information clearly set out

Wotnot Theatre Group

present

The Storm

BY WILLIAM BREAKSPEARE

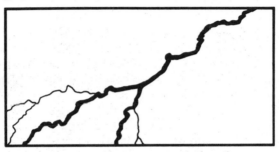

on	Tickets –	
14th, 15th & 16th April 1992	**Adults**	**£2.50**
at The Church Hall,	**Children**	**£1.50**
Fenton	**Concessions**	**£1.50**

A play written for
YOUNG PEOPLE

BOX OFFICE   or 0321 112
Tel: – Fenton 0321 326   or 0321 528

2. A less successful attempt: the design is meaningless and important information about the box office is confusing and difficult to read extension of the lines beyond the frame serves to lead the eye to the details.

Now, the lettering. At least the lettering on both is readable – some posters have elaborate spidery letters, imaginative, elegant and totally illegible. Poster 1 has a consistent typeface, the title stands out clearly and the name of the group and the all-important box office number at the bottom, balance each other well.

But Poster 2 . . . there are nine styles of lettering whose only achievement is to fragment the look of the whole thing. We can see that it is a play written for young people, but you need a magnifying glass to discover the box office numbers. There's another point – one box office number is all you need, three confuses the poor prospective audience. And when does the performance start?

Poster 1 is by no means a 'perfect' poster – there is no such thing – but it serves its purpose well. It attracts, it interests and informs, unlike its feeble sibling. Comparison of these two posters will give you some idea of the fine distinction between effective design and a waste of paper.

Size

Keep an eye open in your area for the size of posters on display, and ask a selection of shopkeepers what they are willing to put up. Some may be reluctant to crowd out their windows with a standard-size poster, but happy to display a more discreet A4 item, so consider splitting your order accordingly.

Don't give up on the big ones altogether. They are invaluable in prime sites such as libraries and railway stations.

Ordering

The number you order will depend on your own requirements and the cost. It is always worth getting a selection of quotes.

Check the lead times your suppliers need, i.e. the time needed to turn artwork into a finished product. Agree a deadline for delivering the finished artwork, and the date when the posters will be ready for collection. And stick to your end of the deal!

Discuss your requirements with the printer and find out precisely what he needs from you. He may be happy to work from the image alone, and to set the lettering himself, or he may need finished artwork, lettering, layout and all. If you do not have a graphic artist among your own contacts, he will often be able to recommend one.

Make sure that the information is accurate, dates, prices etc. There may not be a chance to check the poster before the print run. One mistake, and you could find yourself sitting up till the early hours of the morning with a bottle of correction fluid putting it right!

Display

Aim to have your posters delivered about a month to three weeks before the performance. This gives you time to hand them out for distribution and to cover your area about two weeks before opening night. For a standard production, or concert, it is probably not worth having them up much before then. A more prestigious event, such as a gala night with celebrity guests, or an open-air production, will benefit from earlier publicity.

Stick the posters wherever they will be noticed, newsagents, libraries, colleges, schools, bus stations, hotels, pubs and, if possible, in front of your venue.

A torn and battered poster will be ignored. If the poster is outside, protect it from the elements with the clear sticky-backed film used for covering books. It is also sensible to check key sites every two or three days to make sure that your poster has not been torn down.

Remember that a shop that displays your poster is doing you a favour, so be nice in return. You will have your supporters who will display your material as a matter of course but, if you catch a new site, consider offering complimentary tickets. This costs your group nothing and may gain a new fan. Some shops will display only for a fee. Unless you are desperate for that site it is probably not worth the money.

Don't forget to take your posters down! Tatty posters that hang around for a month after the event are an eyesore.

Keep a record of the sites that you have used, with a note of what size was accepted. This makes it easier to co-ordinate the removal of posters and will save your successor a great deal of footwork. It may save future embarrassment if you keep a list of definite no-go areas too.

Handbills

Handbills are an invaluable weapon in the publicity arsenal. They are a direct route into the hands and the homes of your potential audience, so it is well worth taking time and trouble to get them right. Use them to extend your publicity period, and aim to have them available a month before the show at the latest.

Design

Handbills work well in an A5 format and, for maximum impact, should ideally carry the same image as your posters. However, should your designer be late with the artwork, *don't wait*, sacrifice the picture, and go ahead, using the basic information.

Booking forms

Including a booking form on handbills can be an asset if your group has a wide catchment area. These forms make it possible to order tickets without a special journey to the box office. On the other hand, if your audience is drawn mainly from the immediate locality, you may get little or no response.

There are drawbacks with adding booking slips, in terms of both design and cost. Placing a form on the front of the handbill, below the design and information, can make the whole thing crowded, and hard to read. On the other hand, putting a form on the reverse has the advantage of space and legibility, but will increase printing costs. Wherever you choose to put it, the addition of a booking form attracts VAT.

The form itself should be simple and easy to use. A basic grid with dates and prices is the obvious layout. Make sure that you include the box-office address and the name the cheque should be made out to!

The best way to find out if booking slips work for your organization is simply to try. Experiment for a year, or two – one production is not enough to give you a clear result – and then weigh up the pros and cons.

Distribution

Aim to have your handbills at least a month before a standard production. For a really big event, the time scale should be much earlier, three or even four months ahead.

Handbills have an amazing variety of uses and are relatively inexpensive, so before deciding the quantity it is worth putting some thought into exactly where and how you can use them. Here are some ideas to start you thinking.

Possible outlets:

- Shops.
- Libraries.
- Pubs and restaurants.
- Offices, banks, building societies, estate agents.
- Schools, colleges, evening-class centres.
- Waiting rooms – doctor, dentist, train and bus.
- Public notice boards, etc., etc.

Possible uses:

Substitute for posters Shops that are unwilling to take a poster because of limited window space may be persuaded to display a handbill instead.

Back-up for posters Those outlets that take posters may also be willing to take handbills. Leave them where they will be noticed – a positive 'Shall I leave them here?' may avoid their disappearing into a heap beneath the counter, instead of lying on it.

If you have time, go back and re-stock if necessary. Always make time to collect any that are left once the show is over.

Programme inserts If another group of amateurs in your area is putting on a show shortly before yours, explore the possibility of putting your handbills in their programme. Offer to supply the man-power to do this – they have their own show to worry about and are bound to be short of time and people. Alternatively, ask if you can put leaflets on the seats, or simply leave a pile at their box office.

If they are willing to help in this way, make a point of going to see their production – even better, organize a party. This way you improve your relationship with them, encourage them to come to your show, and check on your publicity material, all at the same time! Be prepared to return the favour and do the same for them next time.

Car stickers Tape a handbill to the side window of a car as an effective alternative to specially printed stickers. Purpose-designed car stickers look professional but can be expensive.

Newspapers Explore the cost of having handbills inserted into Sunday papers. Most newsagents offer this service, but the charges vary, so do your homework and ask around first.

Door-to-door A handbill that arrives with several others in a newspaper has a fair chance of hitting the bin without being read. One that flutters to the floor in splendid isolation may at least attract a second look.

Use a local street directory and select key roads in your area. Then break these into manageable groups, and enlist the help of group members to deliver handbills, preferably close to their own homes. A local youth group may be prepared to handle the delivery for you in return for a small donation.

Mailing list If your group has a mailing list, send handbills out about a month before. Naturally, the postage cost must be budgeted for, but the investment is worthwhile. You are sending out to a pre-selected group of people who have an interest in your performances – the definite maybes! At today's prices, the sale of a single ticket at, say, £3.50, will pay for almost twenty second-class stamps.

Press handouts Always send handbills to the local papers. Take them to your press calls and hand one to the photographer as an additional reminder.

Publicity mornings This concept, which will be discussed in more detail later, presents an ideal opportunity to distribute handbills direct to the general public.

As with posters, keep a list of where your handbills have been placed, and collect the remainder after the show.

Leaflets

Leaflets are expanded handbills. They are more expensive to produce but carry more information and have a longer working life. Leaflets are an obvious publicity tool for festivals and major open-air productions, but they can also work for smaller companies running three or four productions a year.

Tell a story

A well-planned leaflet should read like a short story, with a beginning, a middle and an end. Take a simple A5 format with a single central fold. Page 1 should attract attention and encourage the reader to look further before throwing it away. This is where to put the name of the group, a strong graphic, perhaps your standard logo, and why not set it off with a border of some kind? Pages 2 and 3, the heart of the leaflet, should carry all the information about forthcoming productions. Page 4, the conclusion of your tale, could carry box-office details, perhaps a booking form, general information about the group and a contact for prospective members.

There is an endless variety of formats, sizes and methods of folding – just take a look at the junk mail that comes through your door. Many of your leaflets will be sent by post so always make sure that yours will fit into a standard size of envelope.

Decide on your format, then arrange the information logically in such a way that your 'story' unfolds with the leaflet. Keep the folding pattern simple. The reader needs to be able to fold it back to its original form without taking a crash course in origami. Too complex a pattern and you risk some of the information appearing upside down, or the printer may misunderstand your instructions and the whole thing can be folded in an entirely different way. And watch where the folds come! An awkward fold that hits the middle of a paragraph is bad news. It looks casual and the creased information may be overlooked altogether. If you are in any doubt, always seek the printer's advice.

Seasons greetings

If your group is able to plan productions a year ahead, leaflets are definitely worth a second look. Using them to advertise a single show is overkill but, used to promote a complete season, leaflets can be a valuable addition to your armoury. This type of leaflet can act as a back-drop to your regular publicity drives. It will increase awareness of your activities, and prepare the audience for the next campaign.

All or nothing

The information that appears must be accurate and complete. Titles, dates and venues must all be confirmed before going ahead. If any one of these elements is missing, the leaflet becomes a waste of time and money.

Your group must be certain that, barring disasters, the plays or concerts listed will be produced on those dates, at the stated place. Changing your mind halfway through the year renders the leaflet useless and seriously weakens the credibility of a group. If disaster does strike, it will be up to you as publicity secretary to ensure that the new information, and wherever possible the explanation for the change, is clearly communicated to the public.

The leaflet should also carry an address or phone number for advance booking. If you do not know who will be running the box office in advance, and many groups do not, then there should at least be a contact number where potential customers can get further information.

Use any additional space to attract new members. Give a brief description of the group and its aims, followed by the address and phone number of the membership secretary. Be a little careful about the personal details, particularly if the membership secretary is female. Nuisance phone calls do happen. Consider using only initial and surname, perhaps omit names altogether and print only the phone number. Before using any personal information, either in the press or on publicity material, *always* check with the person concerned.

Joint leaflets

Many areas are served by a variety of amateur groups covering a wide range of the performing arts. All those groups share a need for publicity, and a common target audience. It makes sense to explore the possibility of pooling resources and producing a joint leaflet.

Companions not competitors

Simply talking with other performers in your area is a useful exercise. For one thing, you can go some way to avoiding the dreaded date-clash. Remember you are all chasing the same potential audience – run *The Gondoliers* at one end of the town, a Feydeau farce at the other – and both groups will lose.

There will be heavy competition for poster sites, press coverage, etc. and each publicity campaign will be weakened. This can lead to animosity, resentment and depleted audiences for all concerned. Check your calendars and as far as possible, try to avoid this situation.

Cost effective

The most obvious advantage is financial. Sharing the cost means that each group can afford a better product. The price can come down even further if you can find a sponsor. It is worth making an initial approach to your council and/or arts association.

To get the best value from your joint venture design the leaflets to last. Go for good quality paper and extend your leaflets' useful life by including dates for at least six months ahead, a whole year if you can. An elegant leaflet, packed with useful information, stands a strong chance of being kept for future reference.

3. *A library display, combining a poster with contemporary illustrations and objects to evoke the period and spirit of the play*

Design

The overall design and the number of pages is up to you and your colleagues. Here are a few ideas that I have found useful.

Some form of graphic and a generic title for the front cover will have an immediate impact. The title should make it quite clear what the leaflet is about, a straightforward 'Performance' or 'Wheretown Arts' is fine. Set the productions out in date order. The back cover is an ideal place to include a paragraph about each participating group. Head each piece with the relevant logo and end with a contact number.

Indoor displays

An elegant method of promoting your event is to mount a small indoor display in a public area. Libraries are an obvious choice, but your area may offer other options, such as a community centre, or the foyer of the council offices.

Book your space for the week of the show and the previous week, or even two weeks if you can. Establish how much space you are being offered, and what facilities are available, such as display boards or a table. Then, be creative!

Posters and handbills will form an integral part of the display, but you need that something extra to grab attention. Aim for a three-dimensional display using a combination of the following elements:–

- Photographs and pictures.
- Sketches – of the set, of the costumes.
- Props.
- Costumes.
- Anything else you can think of!

It will save time in setting up and taking down the display if you can prepare the elements of the display in advance, mounted on A4 or A5 cards which can then be attached to whatever display boards are available.

Try to illustrate the key elements in the show, for example, a railway timetable and replica gun for *The Ghost Train*, a Jolly Roger and a truncheon for *The Pirates of Penzance*. The photograph opposite shows a display for *The Royal Baccarat Scandal*. The fan and glove evoke the style of the play, the cards reflect the subject matter, and illustrations give a sense of the period. The central poster is purple on mauve; although elegant, the contrast is not strong enough and the Prince of Wales' feathers motif is lost.

Handbills should be readily available, and it is worth checking and replenishing the supply every couple of days.

3
Billboards, banners, radio and TV

Posters and handbills are the basic tools that no publicity secretary should be without. Let's look at some other, less familiar, methods of attracting public attention to your next production. Think big.

Professional boards

Promotional boards set up on the main roads into your town, provide real impact. These boards are usually produced in conjunction with a local company, often a bank or estate agent. They are prepared by professional sign-writers and carry advertising for your production, together with the name and logo of the supporting organization.

Find your partners

Look out for any similar boards that appear in your district. They will give an initial idea of which companies may be prepared to help. If you are not sure where to go, consider local building societies, banks and estate agents. Perhaps one of them already supports your group by advertising in your programme. Go in and ask.

Find your site

The next step is to establish how many boards the company would be willing to provide, and where to put them. This is not a matter of plonking them down wherever you please, for as long as you want. You *must* have official permission.

If your sponsors have provided boards before, they will know the routine and will advise you who to contact – they may even do it for you. If this is a new venture, you *must* check with the police and the council.

Technically, it is illegal to put anything like this on a public highway and you may be met with a firm refusal. *Never* take a chance and put them up anyway. The consequences could be serious. The boards could be instantly removed and your sponsors fined.

However, if the boards are temporary, i.e. displayed for a maximum of two weeks, and are in support of a community organization, some authorities may be prepared to relax the regulations and allow you to proceed. It is always worth asking.

The local council, usually the highways department, will advise on permitted sites – if any, the size of the boards, and the regulations that operate in your area.

Keep it simple

You want your message to stand out, so resist the temptation to crowd the board with information. Stick with the basics, what, where, when, and how to get tickets.

Say thank you

Your sponsors will obviously benefit from having their name on the boards, but see if there is anything else that you can offer. The more benefit for the sponsors, the more likely it is that they will help you again. Consider offering foyer space for further advertising material – what about a free advertisement in your programme, or at least an acknowledgement? Can you get their name into the press?

Finally, ensure that you offer complimentary tickets, and don't be mean – offer them half a dozen, not just two.

Roadside posters

If you cannot find someone to sponsor promotional boards, it may still be possible to have a roadside display. As with boards you **must** have the permission of the police and the council.

Your standard posters, covered in clear plastic film, could be attached to lampposts, for example. As a strong alternative, make a series of small clear notices, with one piece of information on each. The first carries the name of the production, the second the dates, the third the venue, fourth has the box office phone number. Set up in sequence on a main road, they are easy to read and can be very effective.

Banners

A big, bold banner, say about 30 feet by 3 feet deep, waving across a main street, is a real eye-catcher.

If banners are a regular feature in your area, contact the organizations who use them and pick their brains. Find out what their banner is made of, if you can borrow it and, most important, who to contact for permission.

Getting permission to hang a banner can be a complicated process. Usually you will need permission from the owners of the relevant buildings, and from the local council. All the applications should be made in writing, well in advance of the dates required and all replies should be carefully filed. These documents are confirmation of your time slot should there be a dispute with another organization, and are absolutely essential in the event of an accident.

Safety and insurance must be taken seriously. The situation on liability and insurance must be crystal clear. Make it a routine for one member of your group to check the banner on a daily basis. If the banner tears in a gale, or a rope breaks, you must be prepared to take it down at the earliest opportunity.

Starting from scratch

The precise geography of your town will dictate whether a banner is at all feasible. Ideally, you need a main shopping street that has solid two-storey structures on either side.

Contact the owners of the buildings that offer possible sites for your hooks. Discuss the idea with them and establish that they are willing to co-operate. Discuss the situation with the council with regard to planning and safety regulations.

Once satisfactory arrangements have been made to cement solid hooks into the sides of the buildings, all you need is a banner to hang from them.

Sew or stick?

There are three main types of banner:

- Professionally made with painted lettering.
- Professionally made with stick-on lettering.
- Home-made with sew-on lettering.

Painted lettering

Your telephone directory will supply you with the names of the companies in your area that specialize in making banners. Talk to them by all means, but you will often find that these are 'one-off' banners and are very expensive. The main disadvantage is that the lettering is put on by professional sign-writers, and cannot be changed – not much use to a company running several productions each year.

Stick-on lettering

There are some companies who will create the banner itself but leave the lettering to you. A banner like this can cost around £200, but will last for several years and looks most professional.

Caution: Always ask for details of the type of material that will be used. The material must not be so sturdy that the wind cannot get through. High wind resistance means a high probability that the banner will tear, and even pull the hooks from the walls in the first strong wind.

The company may supply a sturdy variety of sticky-back plastic for the lettering or be able to suggest a source of this material.

Caution: Always ask exactly how you get the letters off. Anything that is designed to stick, while exposed to the elements, is not going to come off easily. These letters are supposed to be easy to peel off after a maximum of two weeks but, left any longer, they become permanent! 'Supposed' is the key word – some of these adhesives are *very* powerful and attempts to remove letters after only a day or two will be met with considerable resistance.

If all your good intentions fail, and the letters stay on for several weeks, the problem is increased.

My own group forgot their new banner, the letters remained for three months and stubbornly resisted any attempt to prise them away from the canvas. The company that had provided the banner, recommended a particularly volatile liquid, and the local chemist kindly obtained it. It took 15 minutes a letter to remove the sticky brown gunge that remained, but the end result was a clear banner. Further experiment showed that white spirit works well for routine removal, but that the procedure still takes time.

Always lay the area of banner to be scrubbed on a hard clean surface. Lay it on a grubby garage floor and the dirt will stick. Soak one letter at a time with white spirit, then peel away the top surface. Scrape the remaining glue with a blunt knife. This soak/scrape procedure will need to be repeated at least once to remove the gunge. The whole of the cleaned area should then be wiped over with white spirit.

Home-made cloth banners

First find a willing victim with a sewing machine! White gauze or net, used double is an ideal material for the basis of a banner. This may not look as smart as a heavy-duty plastic, but it will let the wind through and decrease the chances of wind damage. Allow sufficient room at the top and bottom for a thick rope to go through and sew for strength. Reinforce each end with a strip of canvas, and include a vertical 'pocket' that can take a piece of wood. The wood holds the banner open and reduces the chance of its twisting and tangling in the wind. Banners get extremely dirty, so take cleaning into account in your design.

The letters can be cut out from any old black material. Fraying will not be noticeable from a distance, so don't worry about neat edges. Make sure the letters are secure, and that those that need to, can be taken off again – a regular tacking stitch is all you need – *don't* sew the name of the play by machine. The actual cutting and stitching are time-consuming, so why not hold a 'banner party'? Three or four friends, a bottle of wine, and the job is done in half the time.

Timing

A banner that hangs for too long loses its impact. Aim to hang it the week before your show, and take it down after the last night. Sundays are best for installing and striking your banner – there is less traffic. Always have someone around to keep an eye on the cars and unwary pedestrians.

The ideal 'hanging' team, is a group of three, one with a head for heights and good balance to climb the ladder and deal with the ropes, one to hold the ladder steady, and your 'traffic controller'. And don't forget the ladder!

Important

Boards and banners can provide wonderful high-profile publicity, but they can lead your group into serious problems if they are not properly organized. Any display on a public road is subject to the law of the land, from planning regulations to public safety.

ALWAYS, ALWAYS obtain the relevant permission – and get it in writing. If the powers that be state categorically that such displays are forbidden, then that is the way it has to be. *Never* take a chance and hope nobody will notice – someone will.

Local radio

Local radio stations are another vehicle for getting your message across. The key word here is local. If you are on the edge of the station's range, then it is probably not worth the effort.

It is a help if you are familiar with the programme formats, so that you can target an appropriate show or presenter. Ring the station, well in advance of show time and check on its procedure. Double check that you will be given a free mention, if it is a commercial station, otherwise you may find your piece considered as an advertisement and end up with a bill that you didn't bargain for.

Television

Television is worth a try if you operate in the vicinity of a studio that produces a regional news programme. Again, check the procedure ahead of time. Remember, television is about good pictures, not just information. A particularly strong story, perhaps a celebrity visitor, may attract a news team on a quiet day. You have nothing to lose by asking, and everything to gain.

Mailing list

How often have you heard someone the week after the show, say 'I'd have come if I'd known.' The mailing list is one way of making sure people *do* know. It is an indispensable tool for maintaining contact with all those who have enjoyed past productions and would like to come again. Preach to the converted, and make sure they have no excuse to recant. Your mail shot could simply be a leaflet carrying details of the forthcoming production, or could include a group newsletter.

For a small list, most groups can carry the cost of the postage. Think of it in terms of potential ticket sales. For example, if your tickets run at say £2.50 each, for the current price of first-class stamps you need to sell only one ticket, to cover the cost of ten letters.

However, if your mail service expands, consider the Freepost system, discussed elsewhere in this book (see page 52), or make a modest charge for the service. A small charge not only covers the basic costs but has the added advantage of providing a means of updating a list – no money, no mail shot, no wasted postage.

A mailing list can form the basis of a whole range of schemes: season-ticket offers with special rates, reduced rates for advance bookings, offers of one free ticket per show for regular patrons, and so on and so on. Whether you run such a scheme or a simple list, make it easy for people to join. Put a section in your programme, or leave application forms in the foyer.

Publicity mornings

If the public won't come to you, why not go direct to the public? Personal contact can work wonders. Think about your locality, and identify a site where there is space, and where there are a good number of pedestrians, perhaps a town square, or a wide pavement outside a shop. Then one Saturday morning, before the show, gather members of your group together and get yourselves noticed.

Always make sure you have permission to use the site. Check with the owner of the shop, and/or your local council. It is sensible to talk to the police – nothing is more embarrassing than setting everything up and then being moved on for obstruction.

Dress the part

Encourage group members to wear your sweat shirts, or badges. If you have eye-catching costumes, think about getting a few members of the cast to come in full regalia. I say 'think about' because with our climate it is likely to pour with rain, and you do not want to ruin an expensively hired costume before first night.

Handbills

Give handbills to passers by. Be polite, try saying 'Local theatre', as you wave the paper at them, or they may think you are canvassing for the local election. Children are very good at this job, they love to be involved, and it takes a hard-hearted man to refuse a beaming child.

Be cautious about tucking handbills under the windscreen wipers of parked cars, again you may find you need permission.

Sandwich boards and placards

Ask your back-stage crew to knock together a piece of two-inch-by-two timber with a bit of hardboard, stick a couple of posters on either side, then persuade a couple of unselfconscious members to parade around the High Street. Sandwich boards can be created by sticking posters onto two pieces of strong card – the sides of a large grocery box are ideal. Make two neat holes, an inch or two apart at the top of each side and attach string 'shoulder straps'. The double strap acts as a safety precaution should one tear loose, and makes it less likely that the string will cut into the shoulder of the wearer. Strings at each end of the bottom corners enable you to tie the cards round the volunteer's waist and prevent the boards blowing upwards into their face.

Press

You may be able to combine your publicity drive with a press call. This saves overloading your cast with appointments, and the sight of someone with a camera, snapping away at strangely dressed individuals is a good way to get noticed.

'Spot' prizes

An interesting combination of press and 'on the street' publicity, is to run a spot-the-actor competition. The concept is as follows: the week before your publicity morning, persuade the local press to carry a picture of one of your leading actors, together with the 'challenge'. Members of the public are invited to 'spot' and challenge the target. They will then be asked up to three questions, and the first person with the correct answers wins a prize.

The prize should be attractive, but not too expensive: say a bottle of champagne and, of course, two tickets to the show.

Box office

It is a good idea to set up a small table and have your tickets handy. It is not much use attracting a potential customer and then being unable to cash in on a sale. Make it obvious that you are selling. Have a bold notice saying 'Box office', with perhaps a display board with posters, photographs or press cuttings behind you. A bunch of balloons is a great attention-getter.

Spin-offs

This sort of event helps to make your group an integral part of the local community. Held regularly, people will look out for you.

It also provides an opportunity for your own members to obtain tickets. With the best will in the world, people are basically lazy and, if you save them a phone call, or a trip to your box office, plus an excuse to have a gossip with other members, they are more likely to make the effort.

And what about a ticket-selling coffee morning for group members only? This can be combined with a press call, particularly if the host has a suitable house or garden for photos. If you have managed to strike lucky and have a celebrity, this is a good time to get him or her along for a photograph or two. Many celebrities will prefer a private gathering to being paraded in public.

4
Press releases and photo calls

Good press coverage can make a real difference to your box office, but this aspect of publicity work is often neglected or mishandled. Effective use of the press is not something that can be thrown together at the last minute. Careful planning will make your job easier, and the end result will have more impact.

Homework

Study your market

Read all the local papers to get a feel of their style and make a note of publication days. It is a common practice for there to be several editions of the same paper, so collect editions from other areas and find out which sections of the paper vary. Look out for the free papers and magazines.

Look again

Every publication is different, but most offer more than one opportunity for getting your group noticed. Check for:

- News and features.
- Arts section.
- What's on. ,
- Gossip column.
- District news – often written by a local person.
- Paid advertisement – expensive and, if you do your job, unnecessary.
- Letters page.

Make contacts

One phone call to the editor is not enough. Find out:

- Which reporter covers news in your area.
- Who controls the 'what's on' listings.
- Who is responsible for the arts pages.
- Who compiles the news from the districts.

Phone them, introduce yourself, and most important: *check timing and deadlines*. The best story in the world is no use if it comes in too late.

Timing

Good newspaper coverage can mean the difference between breaking-even and making a profit. As soon as your production is decided, sit down with a diary and work out whom to contact, when to contact them, and the ideal dates for photo calls.

The length of a press campaign and the amount of exposure that you should aim for tend to reflect the size and nature of the event, and the type of audience that you seek to attract. A 'standard' amateur production, if there is such a thing, will always have access to a core audience through personal contact and mailing lists. The press is a means of bringing the show to the attention of those regular supporters who do not have a direct link with the group, and of enticing new people to come and see what you can do. Many of these 'extras' will not buy tickets until a week before at most and often will simply turn up on the night. So, to catch these 'impulse buyers', aim to get your main story in the paper a week or ten days before opening night.

Press coverage for a major event, an open-air production with 500 seats a night to fill, or a charity gala with celebrity guests and expensive tickets, should be run on a different time-scale. These are occasions that your audience will need time to plan for, to organize groups of friends, book a table for dinner, arrange baby-sitters and so on. Give them the time, start the campaign about two months ahead and aim to get a major story in about one month before.

For any event, the 'what's on' listings are vital. This is an ideal way to catch the 'last minuters' who take one look at the TV guide and decide to look for something else to do. If your production is not in their paper, they will not be in your audience.

If you have more than one paper in your district, try to orchestrate your campaign by running different stories on consecutive weeks. Again, one phone call is not enough. Each publication, and often each section within it, will have different deadlines. Free glossy magazines, for example, may work as much as two months in advance.

The campaign

A publicity secretary is effectively the marketing manager of the company – back to soap and cornflakes. You are selling a product and the fact that your product is live entertainment makes no difference to the professional approach that is required.

A manufacturer uses television advertising, you must use the press in the same way. Your production will not be the only attraction on that week, and somehow you have to make it stand out. Make it different, make it interesting, make it memorable.

Newspapers need news, but you have absolutely no right to auto-matic coverage, and there is never a guarantee that what you have told your pet reporter will appear in print. The best you can do is to improve your chances of getting past the editor's reject pile. An editor's job is to sell his paper by providing his readers with interest-ing, relevant articles from the locality. If you want the press to work for you, you must work for them and provide good material.

An all-too-common approach to press coverage is to arrange for one photograph to be taken at dress rehearsal. This is a waste of time. For one thing, this type of shot is often spectacularly uninteresting and stands a good chance of ending up in the editor's waste-paper basket, for another, the picture will be far too late to do you any good. You can do better than that.

With experience, you will work out your own methods, but a useful format for a press campaign has three prongs of attack:

- Information.
- 'Tasters'.
- Photo stories.

Information

Your first move should be to contact the press office at least two weeks before you aim to have your first piece in print. This gives you the opportunity to tell them the basic details and whet their appetites for the stories that you will be offering.

More important, this is the time to begin forging a relationship with the relevant reporters. Always ask the name of the person you speak to, and write it down. There is nothing so irritating as a publicity person who screws up an eager reporter's story by giving the details all over again to somebody else. It wastes time, weakens your credibi-lity and may even prevent your story from appearing.

Take an interest in the way the paper operates – find out which days 'your' reporter is in the office, when are the best times to call and, equally, which times to avoid. It is always worth discovering which day the paper is 'put to bed' – the most exciting story can become a pain in the neck if the reporter is fighting with a deadline.

Make a good job of this first contact and next time you call your contact will remember who you are.

Ensure that each relevant section has accurate details of the event, the dates, the times, the venue, and where and how to get tickets. Always double check, and ask for the information to be read back to you. This sounds obvious, but a wrong date or an incorrect phone number could cost you tickets.

Be prepared to repeat this information *every* time you contact members of the press. They have a lot of other things to remember, and a wonderful story which fails to include the venue and dates of the production is of little use.

Until you are confident that the reporter will get things right, it is wise to confirm all the details in writing. Send a handbill along for good measure, and always, always, keep a copy of your letters.

If, after all your efforts, there is a mistake, see what can be done to rectify it. The paper may be prepared to print a correction. When the box-office phone number is inaccurate, it is worth contacting the 'wrong' number – not only can you apologize for any inconvenience, but the subscriber might be willing to take down the correct number and pass it on for you. While you're at it, why not offer a couple of free tickets as compensation?

'Tasters'

The old saying, 'Tell them what you are going to tell them, tell them, then tell them what you have told them', is certainly true of press coverage. Give the public a taste of what is to come, hit them with a big story and photograph; then, one hopes, round it off with an enthusiastic review.

The first step, is what I call, a 'taster' – the small, but interesting titbits that get your group's name into the papers and pave the way for your main story. A taster is an unusual, funny, or intriguing anecdote which is unlikely to warrant a photograph but is worth a couple of paragraphs.

Every production is different, so use your initiative and see what you can come up with. Keep your eyes and ears open at rehearsals – it is amazing how often a chance comment in the coffee break will lead to a good story. Here are some ideas to get you thinking:

Wanted

Does your production call for an unusual prop? In the past, I have run successful stories asking for such peculiar items as a pair of size-13 slippers and a Russian samovar.

Tell the press what you want and why, making sure you give the title and date of the play, and a phone number to print in case of offers.

If you are really seeking this item, then the director or desperate property mistress may be happy to offer a phone number. On the other hand, if you know that the prop is already in your possession, and you are simply using the idea to get into print, then you would do best to put yourself in the firing line.

Be prepared – however unlikely the item, someone, somewhere, may have it . . . indeed several someones. You could end up with six pairs of slippers and five samovars.

Training

Do any of your cast need to go into training for the role? This can range from getting super fit to play Puck to learning to lie still for *Whose Life is it Anyway*? Do they need to change their appearance? A special hair cut or change of colour makes a good story. And what about weight loss? A well-built gent who is cast to play a starving prisoner in a month's time would make good copy. Does your production call for the cast to learn a new skill, from lace-making to tap dancing?

Get the idea? Good. There are many more opportunities along similar lines – animals, children, costumes, complicated set design. It doesn't really matter. Just be interesting, entertaining, and get your group into print.

Some of these ideas may be suitable for the next weapon in your armoury – the major photo story.

Stop press

Before discussing photo stories and press calls in more detail, a word of caution. The press are out for a good story and do not always take the feelings of those involved into consideration. It is up to you to protect your group and to keep a story under control.

Ask first, print afterwards. Always discuss the idea with the person involved first. *Never* assume that he or she is a good sport and leap for the phone. Not everybody wants his or her name in the papers.

Keep control

Make sure that you are the one the press pester for further details and then you have some control of how much or how little information is passed on.

Never release anyone else's phone number to a reporter unless necessary. If the press want to talk directly to another member of your group, fine. It is a simple matter for you to arrange for that individual to call the paper, rather than the other way round. First, you have an opportunity to brief the interviewee and agree the general line of the conversation, second, it cuts down the possibility of names and addresses being printed indiscriminately.

Protect women members

It is sad but true, that there are people who scan the papers to find a target for abuse. Obscene phone calls are not uncommon.

Some years ago we ran what seemed to us, a perfectly straight-forward photograph of a young woman standing by a table, holding a telephone. The play was set in the 1960s and she was wearing a mini-skirt. The paper printed her name and the district in which she lived. Unfortunately, she had an unusual name, her phone number was easily found in the book, and she had a series of unpleasant calls over the next few weeks.

So, if you run a picture, or a story, which is open to any misinter-pretation of being 'suggestive', make sure that the subject's address is not released. If she, or he, has a distinctive surname, only use a forename. For extra security, use the name of the character being played.

Getting the message across

The ideas are there, you have a great story, now you must decide how to get the details on to the reporter's desk – by phone or letter. When you have established a rapport with your local press, you will find your own balance between telephone conversations and written information. For your first campaign, it is best to telephone first, establish names, deadlines and so on, then follow up with a press release.

Writing an effective press release is not difficult, but like most of the publicity tasks it repays forethought and planning. Your piece of paper is going to land on a desk, covered with a ton of other letters, so make it stand out. Try using coloured paper, preferably with your logo at the top. Light colours are best, they are easier to read, fax and photocopy.

Always type your information. A busy reporter has no time to translate handwriting. Make it easy to read, space it well, and under-line important sections. Keep it simple. Cut out flowery language. Reporters want facts, not a short story.

Don't.

Dear Editor,

After a really long and difficult committee meeting, Wotnot Theatre finally came to the conclusion that it's about time we had a go at something a bit classical, rather than a romping farce or a nail-biting thriller, so we decided our next production is going to be *The Storm* by William Breakspeare.

We'll be doing it in April at the usual place. It should be rather interesting, since the director has got lots of exciting ideas and we will be having music.

Yours

Helen S.

Ouch! This letter is worse than useless. Even if the poor reporter manages to get to the end, it gives him nothing that can go into print. Instead, he is left with the firm belief that Wotnot Theatre is a bunch of amateurs and not worth bothering with anyway.

OK – so I'm exaggerating. That is an example of how not to write a press release – on a grand scale. Let's look at better ways of getting your information across.

Do

- Always include an address and daytime telephone number. The paper may want to check details or get further information.
- Address your letter to the relevant reporter. Passing papers round an office takes time, and there is always the risk that they will get lost.
- Use a bold heading that says immediately what the release is about. Avoid 'gimmicky' headlines – reporters have their own style.
- Get to the point. Keep sentences short and only include information that the general public will find interesting.
- Make the dates, times and venue of the performance clear.
- Include details of ticket availability and how to book.
- Always state the obvious. The reporter may be new to the area and know nothing about your group.

- If you have an interesting angle, use it. Keep the details brief, and never exaggerate – 'unbelievable costume design coupled with a brilliant set'. The audience may not share your enthusiasm.
- Limit your release to one side of a sheet of A4. If more information is needed, the reporter will ask for it.
- Follow up the release with a phone call a few days later.

Now, Wotnot Theatre's press release revisited.

THE STORM
Wotnot Theatre: April 14, 15 and 16

Want to get away from it all? Why not treat yourself to a few hours on a desert island.

Wotnot Theatre Group invite you to enter the enchanted world of Breakspeare's *The Storm* on April 13th 14th & 15th at Wherefore Theatre, Smith St., Fentown.

This tale of magic, betrayal and first love, complete with wizard and monsters, has all the ingredients of a traditional fairy tale. Wotnot Theatre's director, Art Draper, aims to add an extra flavour – science fiction.

With costumes designed and made by the Fentown College of Technology, and original music by local composer, Fred Mozart, this promises to be an exciting production.

Tickets: Price £3, £1.50 for children and OAPs.
Available from The Building Society (next to the theatre).
Curtain up 8 p.m.

For further information please contact:

Felicity Poster: Fentown 1234
or George Banner: Fentown 4321

That's better. The above example is not intended to be an absolutely perfect press release but gives some idea of the type of information to include.

The mention of the costumes and the local composer should spur the press to ask for more details. Don't sit back and assume they will leap to the phone: make a follow-up call yourself. Be ready with suggestions for a photograph to go along with the article.

A photograph which could be used to good effect in the local press

The big one

A good photograph is worth a thousand words. To make maximum impact, you need a good picture. Look at any newspaper; it is the pictures that grab your attention.

Many groups fall back on the posed shot taken at rehearsals, because they have not taken the trouble to think of anything else. These shots are usually dull and, if they are printed at all, rarely get more than two square inches of precious space. You can be different.

The photograph of the small girl with her finger on the actor's lips, actually used as a front-of-house photograph for *A Midsummer Night's Dream*, has good local-paper appeal. Acting with children and animals may be a bad idea, but they do make excellent copy. The setting and costumes reflect the play and the story could be 'Never tell a lady's age', focusing on the girl's debut.

Planning

A successful photo call needs planning. They do not happen by accident.

- Check the deadlines and arrange the date and time at least two weeks before you want the photograph taken. The precise details of the place can usually be agreed nearer the time. Photographers have busy schedules, so avoid changing the location at the last minute, for another one ten miles away – he will not get there in time.

- Check the extent of the geographical area which the paper and the photographer will cover. A perfect setting that is outside their 'patch' will be turned down.
- Check that the relevant people, cast, photographer and host for the location are available.
- Choose your timing so that you do not clash with another major event in your area. Press photographers are often in short supply and heavy demand, so if royalty is visiting your town that day – you lose.

And don't forget regular events such as sports fixtures – Saturday afternoon may suit your cast, but the press are likely to be at the local football match. Saturday morning, on the other hand, is often a convenient time to run a call.

Settings

An original location for your photo call will certainly make your group's name stand out in the photographer's diary. Get to know your locality, and build up a list of interesting buildings, gardens, churches, etc. Get to know your own group's houses and gardens. Find out who has a spiral staircase or a four-poster bed.

Think of an ideal setting for your picture and discuss it with your friends. It is amazing how often you will find someone who knows someone, who knows someone, who has exactly what you are looking for. Wherever possible, do put your cast in costume. It does not have to be the one they are actually going to wear in the play – something that looks right will do just as well.

Period plays

Go for an olde-worlde feel. A black-and-white building, or a garden.

Farce

What about a bedroom? We successfully persuaded a local motel to lend us a room for a couple of hours. It provoked ribald comments, but the press were queueing up! This idea created far more interest than it would have done if it had been set in a private house.

Noël Coward/Oscar Wilde

This style of production calls for elegance. Consider using a stately home, a really 'posh' hotel or restaurant. For *Private Lives*, with my own group, I was lucky enough to spot a 1920 Lamborghini and, with the co-operation of the owner, we gained some very attractive pictures.

Others

Public houses, churches, shops, offices, riverside, children's playground, the list is endless.

Many plays have an obvious setting attached to them – *Outside Edge* calls for a field that can pretend to be a cricket pitch, *Whose Life is it Anyway?* needs a medical setting, so perhaps a local private hospital would help out, *A Midsummer Night's Dream* needs a wooded background, and so on. Use your imagination, and don't be afraid to ask, people can only say 'No', but *always* ask permission beforehand.

Human interest stories

The ideas under 'Tasters' may lend themselves to a major picture. Never ignore the obvious, what is common knowledge to you could be interesting to others. For example, perhaps you have a husband and wife, or a mother and son, appearing in your show. Turn it into a story.

There are interesting variations. One of our most successful press calls was for *Move Over Mrs Markham*. The idea itself was simple. I got out the local telephone directory and contacted a number of 'real' Mrs Markhams. As a result I discovered four delightful ladies who were happy to have their picture taken. In return for their help, we offered complimentary tickets for the night of their choice, and a good time was had by all.

Disasters can help

If your leading actor falls ill, just before the show, this can sometimes be an ideal publicity opportunity. I say sometimes, because these situations need to be handled with tact. Be aware of the feelings of the actor who has been forced to quit. You can cause great distress by publicizing his misfortune.

Consider focusing on the replacement. How long has he got to learn his part? How big is it? Has he acted before?

However you decide to handle the story, **always, always** get the agreement of the parties involved.

Don't ignore the disaster on the night, either. Maybe your lead was struck with laryngitis on the first night, and someone has to go on and read the part at two minutes' notice. It may not help with advance publicity, but it is still a good story, and keeps your group in the public eye. Anyway, the brave soul who goes on deserves some glory.

Celebrity pictures

There is nothing like a famous name for getting the press interested.

Make the connection

For this idea to work, the celebrity must have some link with the production, or with the group. Does your group have a 'name' for a president?

Check the original cast list in the front of your script. Anyone useful there? Keep an eye on the papers, for professional tours in your area. You may find that the same show as yours is on a few weeks before. Is there a 'famous face' in the cast who might be persuaded to help?

Find the agent
Having identified likely candidates, you must then establish their willingness to help, and their availability. Don't rely on writing to them direct, care of a television company; it will take too long for the letter to reach them. You need to make a professional approach through their agent.

The easiest way of identifying an agent is to contact Equity which is usually willing to check its listings and provide the relevant address and phone number.

Make contact
Whether you are making the approach by phone or letter, be crystal clear as to what you are asking the celebrity to do. Outline a number of possible dates, and give the location. The town is probably enough to start with, precise addresses can be given later.

Find out what your subjects expect from you. They may expect an appearance fee, in which case think carefully before proceeding. They may reasonably expect travelling expenses – again check that your budget will cope. If they are willing to give their time freely, find out if they will make their own way, or if one of your group can help with transport. Be clear as to how much time they can offer. They may have to dash back for a matinee.

Be professional
Actors and professional musicians are busy people. They are doing you a favour by offering their services, so treat them with respect. It is up to you to meet them on time, and to run the photo call efficiently.

Make the arrangements clear to the press
It is sensible to confirm the details in writing. If your 'star' only has half an hour, then both you and the press must work within this timescale. It is unreasonable to expect anybody to hang about waiting for a photographer who may or may not turn up.

If the photographer fails to show, be prepared to take a tough line, and sacrifice your story. If the celebrity fails to show, don't disappoint the photographer; have an alternative picture up your sleeve.

A celebrity who learns that you mean what you say may well be prepared to help you out again; mess him about and there is little chance he will come again.

Even without having to work to a tight schedule, a little forethought can save time. Discuss the type of shots with the photographers in advance, or, at least, have a clear idea in your own mind as to what poses would be appropriate.

Resist the temptation to invite all your neighbours and friends to a celebrity call. Keep the occasion quiet and confine the details to members of your group. If time is short, consider restricting the invitation to the relevant members of your cast, yourself, and perhaps the director.

Take the trouble to give basic details to those who are coming. Tell them who the celebrity is, the connection with the play and what he or she is currently doing. This avoids the embarrassing moment when someone trots up to your VIP and happily asks, 'Are you a new member?' or, even worse, the classic 'Hallo, who are you?'

In my own experience, the individuals who agree to help a group in this way, do it because they want to. They come with the intention of spending a pleasant hour or so with people, who like themselves, take theatre and music seriously. Avoid gushing, enjoy their company, and maybe they will be able to help you again in future.

So have a go. Plan your call in detail, and make sure everything happens like clockwork. Ensure that you are there to oversee the operation and leave nothing to chance. If you cannot make it, then someone else who is fully briefed must stand in for you.

Follow up
When you have run a successful call of this kind, be it with a local councillor or a superstar, let the guest see the end results. Collect the relevant cuttings or, if possible, chat up the photographer and obtain prints; then send them to your guest together with a letter of thanks.

Do it yourself
It sometimes happens that you have set up a terrific picture, the paper is keen to have the story, and then the photographer is unable to get to you, either through illness or pressure of work. Don't despair and throw in your resignation – you may be able to save the situation and do it yourself.

This is an occasion when all the groundwork that you have put into building a relationship with the press can really pay off.

If they have confidence in your photo calls and believe that their paper is in danger of missing out on a good picture, first, they are likely to give you as much advance warning as they can, rather than just not appearing, and, second, they will be more receptive to the idea of the group's submitting its own photograph of the event.

Taking pictures from the public is not a popular activity – press photographers need a job, and the average amateur picture is often not good enough for publication. So don't be surprised if they turn down your offer.

If they say 'yes', make sure you are organized. You need to have a good photographer waiting in the wings, armed with a black-and-white film.

Be warned, these days it is difficult and expensive to get black-and-white film developed. Make it part of your general homework to find out where, and how much. You may never need the information, but it is better to have it at your fingertips than to have a mad panic an hour before the press call.

Make it clear to 'your' photographer that he will be doing this as a favour to the group and that it is highly unlikely he will receive any payment for his efforts from the paper. It is also unusual for a name to appear with a picture. Check with your treasurer, and make sure that your volunteer does not end up out of pocket. At the very least, he should be reimbursed for the cost of the film.

Discuss the type of shot required, in some detail and find out precisely how the paper wants the final picture delivered to them, as a print, or a negative, or both. As always, deliver the photograph that you promised, when you promised it, and keep your fingers crossed!

Fair shares

No reporter can resist the word 'exclusive'. Build a reputation for providing interesting copy and you will keep the press on your side. Your chances of getting into print will be enhanced if you regularly offer stories that rival papers do not have.

When you have two or more local papers, try to give each of them something different. Be quite open about what you are doing. The paper will appreciate this individual attention and it may mean the difference between your hitting the front page or the bin.

Even if your photo call for each paper is on the same day and with the same members of cast, always think up a different angle. A good press photographer may well come up with his own ideas – terrific – if they are appropriate to the play, let him go ahead. He will push all the harder to get his own ideas in.

Don't be greedy

You may have several ideas for good photographs, but do not expect that all of them will be printed. The editor does not have unlimited space. Many papers have a policy of sharing publicity between all the performing groups in the area and limit the number of photographs – often down to one per show. This limitation can work for you if you time your calls so that one picture appears in each different paper on consecutive weeks.

Don't be disappointed

There will be occasions, when your call has gone smoothly, the photographer has taken great pictures, and nothing appears in the press. It happens. Ring your friendly reporter and establish the reason. Maybe the photographer missed the deadline, maybe the film was spoiled or lost, maybe there was a major news story and there was simply no space. Check if the picture can be used in the next edition or maybe with the review – better late than never.

The more interesting the picture, the more likely it is to get in. My own group had a near miss when our publicity coincided with a local murder. The paper was full of it. Fortunately, we had had a celebrity guest, and a particularly good set of photos. We were squeezed in because it was a good story.

The critic

Publicity before a show is vital, but the campaign does not stop when the curtain rises. A review (preferably a good one!) keeps the group in the mind of the public. Never assume that, because the editor of the arts page knows about the show, there will automatically be a review. There might be, but critics like to be asked. Find out who they are and invite them to your production. Always offer complimentary tickets – preferably two. Reviewers should not be expected to pay for the privilege of doing their job.

Never tell the cast that there is a critic in the audience. Afterwards is fine; before can play havoc with the nerves.

Look after your critic, but do not fuss. Make sure that he has a good seat, half-way back and towards the centre is a popular place for a reviewer. Box office should know whom to expect and have the tickets ready.

There is no need for you to be there to meet him, and it should be absolutely taboo even to think of sitting next to him. A good critic is quite capable of making up his own mind, without having 'helpful' comments hissed into his ear. Never hover about afterwards, begging for compliments, or worse, to make excuses. The review will be based on the performance that he and the rest of the audience have seen, not about the wonderful dress rehearsal before the lead went down with that nasty dose of flu.

Try to arrange for him to be given a complimentary programme. He will find it impossible to write an accurate review without the names of the players and again, should not be expected to pay for doing his job. One way of ensuring that this happens is to leave the tickets at the box office, and to arrange for a programme to be attached.

Whether the review is good or bad, accept it with good grace. Do not ring up and argue, or write a letter of protest to the editor. What has been printed has been printed. No amount of squirming can change that and will only serve to make the group look thoroughly unprofessional.

In between shows

Publicity for your group can continue whether there is a show or not. It helps to keep the group in the public eye and also to maintain a good relationship with the reporters.

What you release depends on your own circumstances, but remember, what is routine to you could be news. A group car rally, entering a team in a local charity event, a member who has gained celebrity in their own right, might be of interest.

Scrapbooks

Publicity is a nine-days wonder, but it can form a fascinating history of your group. Keep all the press cuttings and build a scrapbook. Include programmes, handbills and reviews, photographs taken during rehearsals and aim to make a complete record of each production.

First, it's fun. Second, a scrapbook can be a source of ideas, for you and for your successors. Third, it gives you something to display to would-be members.

5
Front of house: tickets and programmes

Right, you have successfully sold your tickets, and you have an audience. If your publicity has worked, that audience will include people who have never seen your group before. The task now is to give them a good night out, and make sure that some of them become regulars. Making your audience feel welcome and relaxed is just as important as selling the tickets in the first place. You want them to come again.

Outside

Take a look at the outside of a professional theatre. The building is covered with photographs, posters, reviews, and is ablaze with lights. There is no doubt that something exciting is taking place inside.

Few amateur performers are blessed with a theatre, but you should 'dress' your venue with the same care as your leading lady. If it is at all possible, arrange to decorate your venue a week or so before the production. Your hall or theatre can be a giant poster!

During show week, make it apparent that something is happening. At the very least, put large posters on the building and, if possible, put photographs of the cast outside. There may even be space to hang a banner over the front entrance. New audience members will be able to find you more easily, and, who knows, you may catch someone's eye and tempt them in off the street.

And don't forget the lighting. It is no accident that, when a theatre is closed, it is said to 'have gone dark'. Flashing neon signs are out of your reach, but good basic lighting is not.

Pay a visit to your venue, at night, a couple of weeks ahead of the show and check that the lighting over the entrance, and in the immediate vicinity, is in good working order. If you spot problems, perhaps a street light out of commission, then you have time to contact whoever is responsible and ask for it to be fixed.

Lights make the venue attractive and welcoming, and more important, are vital for basic public safety. While we are on the theme of safety, the outside of the building should be checked on set-up day and all obstacles, litter, broken glass, overgrown weeds and so on removed. You need your audience, and your cast, in one piece.

Inside

Once the audience is inside, they become the responsibility of the front-of-house manager. The following comments are more relevant to him than to the publicity team, but at the same time a scruffy theatre can undo all your hard work.

Take a long hard look at your foyer. Explore ways of making it as attractive and welcoming as possible. Can you put up a display of cast photographs, posters of past productions? Is there anywhere to put fresh flowers? Are there enough rubbish bins? Is the box-office area easy to reach?

The audience may not have set foot in the building before so make sure that the refreshment area, the bar and the toilet facilities are clearly signposted.

Create an atmosphere. If you have the space, and the manpower, think about decorating the venue in a style appropriate to the production. Use your imagination to get your audience in the mood. *The Mikado* begs for a display of Japanese prints, fans, chopsticks, a kimono; *Journey's End* would like a selection of First World War artefacts. Set the tone for a period piece by using appropriate costumes, hats and gloves, and so on. If the actual items are not available, what about paper cut-outs? I saw an excellent foyer display for *The Pajama Game* where the walls were covered with a collage of sewing machines, cotton reels, and dressmaking patterns. (NB You really do spell 'pajama' like that in this context.)

Front-of-house personnel

It is fun to put the programme sellers in costume, though usually neither wardrobe mistress nor budget can run to this. Costume aside, anyone who is dealing directly with the audience, from front-of-house manager, to the lady serving coffee, must look smart. Jeans and T-shirts belong in the rehearsal rooms. Think about a simple 'uniform' of black and white. This may sound a touch pedantic, but it creates a professional image and also makes the 'staff' easily identifiable.

Watch where you position programme sellers. Try to have at least one sales point towards the front of the hall – put them all near the door and you will have an instant traffic jam. If your auditorium is dimly lit, give your ushers torches.

One final word on safety. Accidents do happen. Contact the local

St John's Ambulance and ask for one of their members to be present at each performance. Front-of-house staff and back-stage crew should know exactly what to do in the event of a fire. It is good practice to use a code word or phrase to give the alert. The word 'fire' causes panic.

Refreshments

Refreshments are an integral part of a pleasant evening. They keep the audience happy and can make you a profit. If you have the facilities for running a bar, or making coffee, or both, use them.

A bar is popular but, if you intend to sell alcohol, don't forget about the licensing laws. Contact the local magistrates' court in good time and apply for a licence. Be strict about the people who serve the drink – they *must* be over 18. Obvious maybe, but easily forgotten, and highly embarrassing when a local policeman is among your customers. Check with local off-licences for an indication of prices and the service they can offer. Always go for sale or return. Many of the big chains will provide a selection of glasses. You are responsible for their safe, and clean, return and will be charged for any breakages. When it comes to quantities, the off-licence will have experience to draw on, so ask for advice.

The vast majority of people these days is very conscious of the drink/driving laws. Be fair and provide non-alcoholic beers and soft drinks as well as the booze. One tip, you may well find it cheaper to buy coke and lemonade from the local supermarket. Visit the local cash and carry for canned drinks and confectionery at competitive rates.

Keep your range simple, and put up a clear list of products and prices. It goes without saying that bags of sweets in crinkly wrappers and rustling packets of crisps are best avoided. Keep prices simple: 23p for a bar of chocolate may make you a profit, but giving change for such odd amounts is a headache, and takes time that you do not have in a 15- or 20-minute interval – make it 25p and be done with it.

Swift service is important, so think ahead. Would it be a help to have a number of glasses of wine poured in advance? What about the sugar for the coffee? Is there enough space for people to serve themselves? Should you offer pre-wrapped sugar? Are there enough spoons? Plastic cups may save the washing up but are no substitute for real glass and china.

Tickets

There is more to a ticket than meets the eye. This little piece of paper is:

- A receipt.
- A reminder to the audience.
- A way of checking box-office figures.
- A guarantee of a seat.

Every ticket should carry the time, place and date of performance. It is a good idea to use different colours for each night.

The numbers game

It is always worth numbering tickets in some way, if only to keep track of how many you have sold, and who has taken what to sell at the office. The question is whether they should be reserved or unreserved. Reserved tickets carry a specific seat number; unreserved tickets leave it to the audience to choose where they sit on a first-come-first-served basis. Consider the usual size of your audience. If you regularly play to houses of a hundred or more, then numbered seats are a must. Under a hundred and you may well manage quite successfully with an unreserved system.

My own organization uses a combination of both systems. Evening performances are well attended and have reserved seats, but we use unreserved tickets for our Saturday matinee when audience figures are much lower.

Format

After that, you must then choose the style of ticket. There are two basic types, the simple piece of card, or the tear-off variety. Most local printers will be able to come up with a basic card ticket. Notice, I said 'card', not 'bit of paper'. It may not be possible to have the numbers printed, but it is not difficult to do this by hand. As usual, shop around for quotes.

Tear-off tickets come in booklets with two, three, or even four detachable sections. There are a number of companies who specialize in this type of ticket. They use a computerized system so delivery is usually quick and prices competitive. (See Appendix: Useful addresses.)

Three-part tickets are probably the most useful. The stubs left in the book give you the number of tickets that are 'out on the street' before the show, the section surrendered at the door gives you an accurate audience figure on the night, and the third section, retained by the public, means that people can find their seat and have the evidence to settle any dispute as to who should be sitting where.

Four-part tickets can be very useful for giving your audience a form of currency on those occasions when you include a 'free' drink, or a meal, or even a raffle.

For a low-budget show with a small audience, it is possible to abandon tickets altogether and work on a system of admission by programme.

Ordering

Order your tickets well in advance of your main publicity. There is nothing worse than being asked for tickets and having to say that they are not available for another couple of weeks. That is a sure way to lose custom.

When ordering reserved tickets, make sure that you have access to a seating plan complete with letters and numbers. A printer specializing in tickets will be able to work from this and set the numbers by computer. For a smaller printer you may have to write out a complete list.

You need a copy of the plan, and so does the front-of-house manager – someone has to label the seats. And make sure that those labels do not part company with the seats.

Pricing

How much you charge for tickets is a decision for the group's committee. As a basic rule, you should always aim to make a profit. Check your pricing with an educated 'guesstimate' of how much the show will cost, and how many 'bums on seats' you are likely to get.

For example, if a show costs £1200 to put on, and your average audience for the week is 500, including about 100 children at half price, then charging £3.00 and £1.50 will result in takings of £1350 and will only just cover your costs. Don't take the risk – £3.50 and £2.00 is a much safer option.

Box office

Make it easy to get tickets

The world's best publicity campaign will be entirely wasted if tickets are not readily available. Potential points of sale are:

- Personal contact.
- At the door on the night.
- Local shop/business.
- Telephone booking.
- Mailing list.

Personal contact

Friends, relatives and work colleagues are a prime source of ticket sales for any amateur group. Encourage all your members to carry handbills around with them as a matter of course. When the forth-coming show comes up in conversation, many people who express an interest either have not got their diaries to hand, or need to talk to their other half, or book a baby sitter, and then they forget all about it – don't let them! Give them a handbill to take home and keep your fingers crossed.

Resist the temptation to hand everyone in the cast ten tickets for a selection of nights and tell them to sell. This causes chaos. Box office will have no idea whether tickets are actually sold, or sitting in a handbag. Some people will want three for Friday, instead of Wednesday, and 'By the way, can I change this Saturday one for an aisle seat?', etc., etc. I told you – chaos. If tickets are not returned before the appointed night, you may turn people away at the door, only to find a row of empty seats when the curtain goes up.

Then there is the awkward matter of extracting the money. It is not easy to badger friends for cash, and if, as is sensible, you expect any tickets not returned after say, two days before the show, to be paid for, you have to ask a harassed member of the cast to cough up. Not easy.

It is much better to issue tickets only against firm orders, or to arrange for them to be collected and paid for on the night.

On the night

Take a leaf out of the professional theatre book and, space permitting, consider setting up two box-office points, one for impulse buyers, the other for reservations. It is important that the box-office manager has an efficient system for dealing with the reservations. It looks very unprofessional to rummage about in a shoe box for the relevant tickets. 'I'm sure it's here somewhere' will not please the customer, nor the queue of people behind him.

Local shops

Your publicity should be all over the town, and it makes sense for the tickets to be there too. Approach a local estate agent, travel agent, building society or bookshop, and ask if they would be prepared to act as a booking office. Offer them a commission, say 10 per cent of their ticket sales, and point out that they will have the benefit of extra bodies walking into their shop.

Timing

Don't release all of your tickets for all of the time. You need easy access to the tickets for your cast and your mailing list. Fix a date to take them to the shop about three weeks before the show. Ensure that this date is displayed on your publicity material and stick to it.

Telephone booking

This method is becoming increasingly common, but is not always well managed. The obvious, but often forgotten rule, is that the phone number that appears on your posters etc, must be manned. Potential audiences are fickle and, if they make three attempts to book tickets and still get no answer, they will give up.

There are two ways round this: stipulate opening times and/or use an answering phone.

If the number given belongs to someone who is out during the day, state a specific time, 6–9 p.m. Then *be* there! Answering machines are invaluable. Consider purchasing one for the group. When not in use by box office, I guarantee the secretary, or the chairman will find a use for it.

An answering-machine system will not solve all your problems. There will be queries that require a person, not a machine, to respond. Again, consider stating a specific time for personal queries on the message tape. Any message that needs a response, must get one within 24 hours.

Credit cards

For the average amateur company, credit cards are a great idea, but not economically viable. This method of payment comes into its own for a really big event that attracts an audience from outside the immediate locality. To give you some idea, one company that presented an open-air production, and played to an audience of over four thousand, found that almost half their mail-order customers chose this method of payment.

So, how do you do it? First, contact the group's friendly bank manager and make enquiries. At the time of writing, the bank is likely to charge 4–5 per cent on each transaction, and it will cost between £60 to £100 to set up an account. The bank will provide the 'kit'. The machine, the stationery and an instruction booklet.

Credit-card booking looks professional and your audience will pay for the convenience. This means that the expense can be offset by charging a small booking fee – say 75p per transaction.

Mail order and Freepost

If you have a mailing list (if you haven't, you should have!), you need to make it easy for the recipients to get tickets. They can telephone, and perhaps pay by credit card, but they should also be able to fill in a booking form and send a cheque.

Decide whether tickets reserved in this way will be sent direct to the customer or left at the box office. The box-office system is cheaper. If you send the tickets by post, consider asking for a stamped addressed envelope with each order.

Think for a minute – can you lay your hands on two envelopes and two stamps? I suspect that for at least half of you the answer will be 'no'. The Freepost system can help. The current annual cost of a Freepost licence is £27.50, plus a handling fee of ½p per item, plus postage – first or second class. Naturally, you pay postage only on the replies that you get. As with credit-card bookings, it is a question of economics and the number of tickets you aim to sell. The Post Office will send you details and an application form.

Programmes

Programmes are an amazingly flexible item. They can be as simple as a photocopied sheet of A5, or as elaborate as a 16-page glossy brochure complete with photographs. The choice is yours.

Cover

Apart from the obvious, the title of the play, the author and the price, the cover needs some form of graphic. Use the logo of your group, or the design that was employed on your posters, or both.

Contents

At the very least, your programme should carry a cast list, back-stage credits, details of the action of the play and the time and length of the interval. Additional items could be:

- Who's who.
- Producer's notes.
- Photographs.
- Previous productions.
- Advertisements.
- 'Fun' items – puzzles, articles, etc.
- Acknowledgements.
- Group information.

Who's who

An audience enjoys a 'look behind the scenes' and knowing a bit more about the performers. Regulars will get a kick from saying 'I thought he looked familiar, I saw him in such and such ', or 'Good heavens! It says here, she was in so and so, I'd never have recognized her.' You can choose to give a straight informative biography, very much on the lines of a professional programme, stating the actor's previous roles and experience, and a snippet about his private life, his job, his hobby, or the fact that he has sixteen cats and a goldfish.

If you have space, think about making the entries entertaining as well as informative. Perhaps some of the cast are related, if an actor is playing a DIY expert and doesn't know one end of a screwdriver from the other, or perhaps he played the victim in a previous play and is now the villain of the piece, the possibilities are endless.

Some plays lend themselves to a theme running through the biographies, for example, each has a remark about cooking, home improvements, cars, and so on.

For my own group's production of *Adrian Mole*, all the actor's notes had a 'school report' at the end. The 'biog' for the actor who played Adrian's father, George Mole, came out like this:

> Best known to regular audiences for his comedy roles in *Habeas Corpus*, *Move Over, Mrs Markham* and *The Unvarnished Truth*. As father of two young sons, he hopes his role as George is not a rehearsal for things to come!
> Music history: Jim Reeves *is* dead.

You can even have a joke with the audience. We ran one programme, where every biography gave the actor's age as 33 regardless – it was amazing how long it took some of the audience, even some of the cast to spot that one!

Unless you know your group really well, it is best if you ask the performers to write their own 'biogs' and give you the details in good time. You can then sit down, and tidy them up. It is good policy to make sure that each entry is about the same length, that your information is accurate, and that you've spelled all the names correctly.

Producer's notes

This provides an opportunity for the producer to express his/her feelings about the play and to put the audience in a receptive mood for what they are about to see. It can be light-hearted or serious and include the history of the play, the reasons it was chosen, the fun in rehearsals, anything.

As with the biographies, give your producer an indication of the space available, and let your producer get on with it. It should be understood that you, as editor, have the final say. Never let the producer's notes be apologetic or offer excuses for the play or the standard of performance.

Previous productions

A self-explanatory item, but, as with the 'Who's who', it provides an opportunity for your regular audience to feel involved with the group and acts as a shop window to newcomers, giving them a sense of the range and style of productions of your group.

Photographs

Good pictures can really dress up a programme, smudgy grey photos can wreck it, so always check with your printer as to feasibility and format. Usually a good-quality black-and-white print will do the job. Again you can choose between group pictures, the backstage crew, rehearsal shots, or head-and-shoulders portraits of the cast. The latter look very good next to the biographies.

Remember, these pictures can work for you. Blow-ups can be used to decorate the front of your theatre, or the foyer. Keep a library of portraits, a 'rogues gallery' of your actors, and use them next time they appear.

Puzzles and articles

These items can be useful, but make sure that they fit the style of your programme and the production; don't shove them in for the sake of it.

Acknowledgements

Everyone likes to be thanked. Use your programme to thank local shops or companies who have been particularly helpful, from the one who provided your hoardings to the shop that lent you a basket of silk flowers, or a stone frog.

Group information

The programme can usefully carry names of the membership secretary, the contact for joining the mailing list, perhaps the contact for the hiring of lights, costumes, scenery, etc. It is excellent practice to include the dates and title of the next show – if you know it.

Advertisements

Advertisements mean money. They can cover the cost of your programme, or make a healthy profit. Work out the style of your programme, and the number of pages that you can usefully fill with information about your group, then decide what proportion of the programme can be offered for advertisements.

Never overload a programme with them. Faced with ten pages of advertisements and only two about the group, the audience will feel cheated. A 60/40 ratio of advertisements to group information is about right, so in a twenty-page format, you can allow twelve pages for advertising.

Think about where you intend to put the ads: scattering them between group information pages can make the selling space more attractive than if you lump them all together at the back. The advertisers hope that at least somebody will read them.

Next sit down with your treasurer, a bottle of wine and a calculator, and work out the costings. Take into account the cost of printing, the charge you intend to make for the programme, and consider what you can reasonably expect to charge your advertisers.

Never undersell advertising space but, on the other hand, don't put your prices so high that no one will buy it. Remember that most local firms place an advert as a form of donation to your group. Yes, it keeps their name in the public eye, but they do not expect a major return.

If your group runs more than one production a year, think about selling space for the whole season, rather than for one production at a time. This has three main advantages: the printer can carry the artwork from one production to the next; your prices can be adjusted to give a discount for a whole-season booking; it saves an amazing amount of time and energy in selling and chasing copy from the advertisers.

Aim for a minimum of £50 per page, perhaps split into £45 for a full page, £25, for a half page, and £15 for a quarter. And don't underestimate the attraction of a back page. This is a prime spot, and perhaps you could sell that at a premium, say £75.

My own group runs the ads across three programmes a season, and we currently charge, and get, £100 per page, £50 per half, £30 per quarter, and £125 for the back cover.

Once you've finished scratching your head and chewing your pencil, it is time to move to the telephone, and sell.

Selling

Start early. July is not too early to start selling for a season that begins with a production in late October. Advertising budgets for most local businesses are limited and disappear fast. In any case, the advertisers may need time to prepare their copy, and you have a printer's deadline to meet.

Arm yourself with a dummy copy of your proposed programme, so that you can mark off the sold spaces. This is easier than keeping a list. You are less likely to make a mistake and sell the same page twice if you can see it in front of you.

Take a local telephone directory, programmes from other groups in the area who carry ads, a local paper, even the parish magazine; all these will give you an idea of whom to contact.

Have your price list in front of you, and also the number of programmes that you intend to order and an indication of your average audience figures. Your advertiser will want to know what he is going to get for his money.

Keep a careful note of what you sell, get the name of the manager, or the person you are dealing with, and check on the precise address of the establishment. Discuss the style of the ad. Are the advertisers happy to leave the lay-out to you? Will they provide their own artwork?

If you are successful, be very, very clear with your purchasers as to the deadlines. You have a programme to get to the printers. You cannot afford for one advertiser to mess you about and miss the vital date as a result. Tell them that copy is wanted by such and such a date, remind them if necessary, but, if it comes to the crunch and their copy is too late, then it does not go in.

Be business-like

Design a simple form of invoice which confirms the name of the company, the space bought and the cost. Include the name of your treasurer, or the address where the money should be sent. Keep a copy for your own records. The existence of some sort of invoice often makes it easier for the company to authorize payment and, important for you, speeds the whole process of collecting in the cash.

It is a good idea to send a copy invoice after the show, together with a sample programme, so that the advertisers can see what they are paying for.

The proof of the programme is in the reading

When the proof arrives from the printers, check it carefully. This is your last opportunity to alter anything. A programme that is full of mistakes looks unprofessional and will do nothing for the image of your group. Use a ruler and go through every word, particularly phone numbers in the advertisements. Don't just flick through. The human mind has a tendency to see what it expects to.

THE NEXT PRODUCTION WILL BE THE
THE FAMOUS MUSICAL 'STOPPING OUT'

Well, I expect you would catch that it should be 'STEPPING', but did you spot the extra 'THE'?

6
Charities and sponsors: gala and open air

The tasks of organizing a charity event or seeking sponsorship often fall into the lap of the publicity secretary. Whether you are aiming to take financial support, or give it, charity and sponsorship can both lead to a higher profile for your organization and bigger audiences.

Charity

First, find your charity. There are so many worthwhile causes in need of funds that you can find yourself spoilt for choice. Select the charity that you believe will have the greatest appeal to your audience. This may sound selfish, but remember, in order to make a significant donation, you need to sell those tickets.

Members of the public are more willing to give if they are clear how their money will be spent. It is therefore worth considering a big national charity that will attract unquestioning support or, at the other end of the spectrum, a smaller organization that is well known in the locality. You don't need to stop at one. Give the lower-profile organizations a chance by supporting them at the same time as a charity with a 'strong' image.

The nature of the performance may lend itself to a specific charity; *One Flew Over The Cuckoo's Nest*, *Duet for One*, *The Miracle Worker*, all fall into this category.

The donation

How much you choose to give away, is entirely up to you. It is logical to tie the amount of your contribution directly to the profits of the production. This encourages the charity to go out and sell tickets, in the knowledge that it will reap the benefits. It also means that the group will not find itself out of pocket or, worse, unable to afford the promised donation.

Here are four of the most useful ways of arriving at the final figure:

- Offer a percentage of all tickets sold.

- Offer the total profit.
- Run one performance specifically for charity, and donate all monies received on that night.
- Offer a specific number of free tickets that the charity can sell at face value, or at a premium.

Whatever you decide, make a clear agreement with your chosen organization in advance.

On the night, offer display space for the charity's own publicity material in the foyer. Consider placing collecting boxes near the box office and the refreshment area. It is amazing how loose change adds up. It is also worth allowing charity personnel to circulate with boxes in the interval. Be careful not to overdo the number of 'opportunities to give'. Don't harass your audience into parting with money – neither you nor the charity will benefit in the long run.

The reward

Your reward should be increased ticket sales. Many people who would not think twice about coming to your performance may be persuaded to buy a ticket to support a good cause. Once they have seen how good you are, some of them will come again.

Liaise with your charity and obtain permission to use its name and logo on your publicity material. Encourage the charity to sell tickets to its regular supporters. Don't expect a landslide from this source, but you should gain a reasonable number.

Ask the organization to advertise your show in its newsletters and magazine, if it has one. It may also be willing to promote the show at its own events.

The press

Good causes make good copy. Include details of your link with the charity in your press campaign. Always discuss your plans with the organization first and double check any factual information. More often than not the charity will be delighted with the extra publicity, but it will not be so pleased if the press report is inaccurate.

Maximize the column inches for your group and aim for a follow-up story. Provide the press with details of the amount raised and, if you can arrange some form of cheque presentation, this should tempt the photographers.

Think big. The press love the giant cheque. Simply contact your local bank and ask for an outsize version. There should be no problem, and usually no extra charge. The bank will ask for a normal-size cheque to go through the system and provide a giant dummy for the ceremony.

Gala evenings

The secret of a successful gala is in the image. What does the phrase 'gala performance' mean to you . . . glamour, style, quality, wealth, exclusive, champagne? All those things are part of the package you must put together, tie up with satin ribbon and sell to the audience.

By definition, a gala performance is not something that happens every day of the week. It is, of course, possible to run a gala evening for every production, but to my mind this devalues the concept. Keep galas special and use them sparingly to celebrate a specific occasion – to promote a major charity, to mark an anniversary in the life of your group or in the life of your town.

Choosing the day

A gala performance may be a one-off performance but is often one particular night during the run of a production. There is no right or wrong answer as to which day of the week you should choose, but it may be helpful to take the following points into consideration.

> *First night:* this carries all the associations of glamorous first-night parties in the professional theatre. *But* will your cast be ready? Remember, you are aiming at quality entertainment. For many groups, a first night has an air of panic and uncertainty. Nerves will be on edge anyway, and the added pressure of a gala may lead to mistakes and a second-rate performance.

> *Mid-week:* apart from a first night, the choice of Monday to Thursday has little to recommend it. Your audience will be tied to the work routine – they have to rush to get to the theatre, they have to get up early next morning and are less willing to stay out late. In other words, they will not be able to relax fully and enjoy themselves.

> *Weekends:* Friday and Saturday are the classic choice. Sunday can also work well, particularly for an open-air performance where there is the possibility of a picnic beforehand.

Whichever night of the week you consider, take the patterns and traditions of your group into account. The planning team should ask itself the following questions before deciding:

- In terms of ticket sales, should you aim to boost your weakest night, or capitalize on your best seller?

- If you select your strongest night, and intend to donate the proceeds to charity, will you make enough profit the rest of the week to break even, or are you happy to make a loss?

- Who are your target audience? Are you aiming to attract new blood, or concentrate on your regulars? If you select the night that is usually heavily supported by friends and relatives, will they still come, even with a higher ticket price. Will they change their night, or will you lose them from this production altogether?

- Does your group traditionally have a cast party on that night? Will they mind sacrificing it?

Go for the glamour

Your gala audience must be made to feel both privileged and pampered. Ticket prices will be higher, but so will the audience's expectations – you must not only create an aura of glamour and style, but deliver a quality product.

Tickets

Ticket prices can set the tone for the evening. Be realistic, but never sell yourselves short. There is nothing out of the ordinary about paying £3.50 for an evening at the local theatre; charge £10 and it begins to feel special. Think about the precise figures. You are selling a luxury product not a bargain – £13.65 may effectively cover the costs but sounds like a price tag in a January sale: charge £15.

The ticket itself should look expensive and be easily distinguishable from your usual format. Go for card, rather than paper, make it larger than usual, and take trouble when choosing the typeface. A ticket that is designed to look like an invitation will add to the sense of occasion.

Programmes

Again, you can move the evening out of the ordinary by planning a glossy souvenir programme. The additional expense of printing can be offset by increasing the cost of advertising space and raising the price of the programme to the audience.

An advertiser will be willing to pay more to be included in an elegant programme that is likely to be kept for future reference than in a basic version that will be thrown away the next morning; £100 per page would not be an unreasonable target.

The audience will appreciate a well-presented souvenir of a memorable night out – £2.00, or even £2.50, should be acceptable.

Refreshments

Consider including the cost of refreshments in the ticket. This can range from a glass of wine in the interval to a three-course meal before the performance.

Be careful to maintain the 'quality' image and think more in terms of champagne and canapés, rather than coffee and biscuits.

Any form of refreshment that is offered 'freely' will make your audience feel like honoured guests rather than common customers. They will feel pampered, which is exactly what is required.

Celebrities

The opportunity to rub shoulders with the rich and famous will add glamour to any occasion. Send out invitations to celebrities well in advance, and aim to have the majority of the replies before your publicity material is finalized. An event advertised as a 'Grand Celebrity Reception', at which the most famous person turns out to be the local vicar, would be extremely embarrassing.

Make it clear in your invitation exactly what you expect from your 'stars'. Will you be expecting them to pay for their ticket, sign autographs, make a presentation, attend a reception as a guest of honour, or just to be there?

Front of house

The glamour of the evening itself is all important, and attention to detail will pay off. The front-of-house staff should be in formal evening dress. The foyer should look as elegant and expensive as possible; think about using fresh flowers, pot-pourri, drapes, perhaps a red carpet.

All these items can eat into your budget, so it is worth approaching local retailers and seeking donations in kind. In return, you can offer the opportunity to display their products. For example, a florist may be willing to provide the flowers, in return for having the firm's name displayed beneath each arrangement.

Sponsorship

Sponsorship and charity work are two sides of the same coin – only this time the coin falls into your pocket. Both these aspects of publicity involve a two-way partnership with another party.

As a working definition, sponsorship is the process of obtaining support in return for an advertising opportunity. Any company who buys an advertisement in your programme can be seen as a sponsor. There is the mistaken belief that sponsorship is complicated and too difficult for many groups to tackle. The truth of the matter is that the degree of work involved largely depends on how much you hope to gain from the deal. The more money you expect from your sponsor, the more effort you will need to put in.

Types of sponsorship

The most usual arrangement is to seek support for a specific production, but it is not the only one. Think about the component parts
of a show – perhaps this time you could look for help with the
costumes, with paying for the programme, for providing the biscuits
– the possibilities are endless.

Sponsorship in kind

Support does not always have to be in terms of hard cash. Anything
that saves your treasurer from pulling out his cheque book is a form
of sponsorship. A local electrical company may be willing to provide
that much needed light or fit it for free. A textile company could be
asked to provide the material for those elaborate period costumes.

One group that I know were having a hard time tracking down a
large table – they approached a furniture company, who not only
provided the item, but delivered and collected it free of charge.

All you have to do is to ensure that such generosity does not go
unnoticed: a free advert in the programme, a story in the local press, a
display in the foyer, will give your benefactor publicity.

Sponsoring a production

A well-planned presentation and a professional approach will increase your chances of success.

In today's economic climate, businesses have neither time nor
money to waste and there are many other organizations chasing after
limited funds. Think and plan carefully before you make the first
contact; you may not get a second chance.

The initial approach

It is not easy to find a willing sponsor. Do not be disheartened if you
fail to strike lucky on your first attempt. Draw up a list of at least a
dozen likely prospects and be prepared to work through them.

A word of warning, don't attempt to contact them all at once, for
unless you are supremely well organized this can lead to confusion.
On the other hand, writing to only one, and then waiting for a reply
before moving on to the next, can take weeks. Time is something that
you do not have. Compromise and target prospects in batches of
three or four.

It is worth aiming for local companies, or at least local branches of
national organizations. Your offer of an advertising opportunity will
be that much more attractive if your catchment area for publicity
matches theirs.

The first thing you need is the right contact. A letter that is vaguely
addressed to the managing director is not enough. If you do not have
a name, telephone the company and find out. Check the person's

title, name and initials, and also confirm that you have the correct address.

Then write a *brief* letter, outlining the nature of your group, explaining that you are seeking sponsorship for the next production, and giving an indication of what is in it for them. Ask for a meeting in the near future, and make sure you give clear instructions on how you can be contacted. Avoid naming a sum of money at this stage, and don't worry too much about the details – the company will either be interested or it won't.

The meeting
So far so good, the company is interested, you have your appointment. Now you must convince it that this is a worthwhile proposition.

You are dealing with business people, so speak their language and be businesslike.

The presentation
The best way to get the information across is to develop a 'sponsorship pack'. This provides the manager with evidence of the style of your operation, makes it less likely that you will forget a significant piece of information and gives him something tangible to take away for further consideration and discussion.

The sponsorship pack could include:

- Samples of previous handbills/posters.
- A programme.
- Reviews of a past production or two – if they're good ones.
- Press cuttings and photographs.
- Details of any other relevant publicity method.

The offer
Advertising through normal channels is expensive – offer your sponsor value for money, and a range of promotional opportunities.

Publicity material: including the company logo, and 'Sponsored by . . .' on handbills, and posters, will give your sponsor valuable publicity and should not cost you a penny extra.

Programme: the sponsor's name should appear, at least once, in a prominent position in the programme. Offer a full-page advertisement free of charge. The most valuable position is on the back cover.

Press: offer to use the sponsor's name in all your press releases.

Foyer display: if you have the facilities, offer the opportunity of a display in the foyer, or at the front of the theatre.

Tickets: offer a number of free tickets, and/or a discount rate.

Social: offer an opportunity to 'meet the cast' and provide a glass of wine.

The agreement

Once the sponsor has decided to work with your group, it is important that both parties understand exactly what each expects of the other.

The amount of money involved depends on individual circumstances, but you should have an agreement as to when the cheque will arrive – before or after the performance, or half now and half later.

Deadlines are vital. The sponsor should be made fully aware of any artwork deadlines involved. Anticipate problems and give him a submission date, a week or ten days ahead of the 'real' one. The sponsor must understand that if his artwork is late, then it will not be included. Obviously you will do your best to fulfil your side of the bargain; after all, you want the money. On the other hand, you cannot be expected to jeopardize the publicity for the whole production.

In a similar manner, the sponsor should appreciate that although you will undertake to mention the company's name every time you contact the press, you have no control over what will actually be printed.

Agree how many free or special-rate tickets will be made available and arrange the details of any front-of-house display – when it can be set up, and who will do it, etc., etc.

Then *put it in writing*. The company will appreciate your professional attitude and a detailed letter of confirmation can save a great deal of argument should anything go wrong.

Open air

Running a publicity campaign for a major open-air production is the promotional equivalent of running a marathon. Everything is bigger, glossier and more expensive. Open-air theatre is no longer a simple box of washing powder or cornflakes, but a luxury item made with the finest-quality ingredients, wrapped in cellophane. The high costs of mounting an event in the great outdoors, mean that you must sell a significantly higher number of tickets to cover the expenses. On the other hand, you have more to offer the paying public.

Your campaign should make the most of all aspects of the performance and reflect an image of sultry summer evenings, elegance, culture and style.

The main attractions
The play
The play that you choose to perform sets the tone of the occasion and has a major impact on your box office, so choose with care. Shakespeare is perhaps the most popular choice for open-air theatre; his plays call for large casts, wonderful costumes and are full of spectacle. There are others, but not many, that fulfil the requirements so exactly.

Location
A good venue can be worth a thousand tickets. The location is the most important element in the open-air-theatre recipe. Look for an attractive setting, picnic areas and good car-parking facilities. There is rarely any choice. A suitable venue either exists in your area, or it doesn't.

Capitalize on the surroundings in words and pictures. The public should not be allowed to forget that this is open air, something special and not to be missed. Every photograph that appears in the press should be taken outdoors, either in the actual setting, in a garden, or the local park. Include a brief description in the leaflets – 'idyllic setting of . . .', 'on the lawns of . . .' rather than the name alone.

Make sure that the audience know where to go. The catchment area for this type of production may well include people who are unfamiliar with the local geography. Print directions and/or a map on the tickets.

The timing
Weekends are the best sellers. The audience has time to relax, to bring a picnic, and to enjoy an attractive venue before the performance. So give serious consideration to running a Sunday performance. It will cost little extra; after all, hired costumes and lights are usually booked out till the Monday. For the same reasons, it is also worth considering whether it would pay to run the play over two weekends, say Thursday to Sunday – the cast needs a break in the middle.

Seating
Rain, or the idea of rain, can put people off. If you have arranged for covered seating, make a point of saying so in your publicity material.

Catering

The opportunity to enjoy good food before the performance in idyllic surroundings can be a key selling point. Go for something more than tea and sandwiches. Reinforce the image of elegance with strawberries, cream and a glass of wine served from an elegant marquee.

Look into the possibility of serving a three-course dinner. If your location has a picnic area, think about providing a hamper complete with wine. The demand for dinners and hampers is impossible to predict, so turn this to your advantage. Include an order form on your leaflet. This gives you the opportunity to list a tempting menu, and whet the audience's appetite.

Creating this mouth-watering prospect is only practicable if high-quality refreshments can be delivered on the night. It is wise to avoid a do-it-yourself approach, and to go to the professionals. If the caterers are well known in the area, coming perhaps from a local restaurant, that gives you an added selling point.

Toilets

Not something to make a song and dance about on a poster, but absolutely essential. Hiring temporary toilet facilities is not difficult, and remember that an audience that has felt uncomfortable, or embarrassed will not come again.

The Campaign

The tools of the trade are, as always, posters, press, leaflets and so on. The differences between this campaign and one publicizing a standard production lie in the quality, the quantity and the time scale involved. Think about your target audience for a moment. The bulk of your tickets will be bought by professional people, over 25, probably with a high income and socially active.

Quality is vital. This type of audience is happy to pay over the odds for an evening out, but will expect a high standard of entertainment in return. The quality of the publicity material must create these expectations.

The paper you choose is important. Go for a reasonable thickness for handbills and leaflets. Flimsy paper looks cheap. If you can afford it go for glossy paper. Think of the impression created by a glossy magazine in contrast to its weekly counterparts.

The colour matters too. Be bold and choose positive colours, red and black, deep blues and purples. Two colours are better than one, and don't overlook the possibility of gold and silver for a real touch of luxury.

Programmes

Programmes can move up market and should easily pay for themselves. A stylish souvenir programme will sell for a minimum of £1;

even £2.50 may not be unreasonable. Think big, move into an A4 format and make it interesting. Include photographs of the cast, the setting, previous productions, an article on any associated charity or key sponsor.

Advertisements are essential to the finances, and the bigger and more prestigious the event, the more willing a company will be to buy the space and the more you can charge!

Handbills and leaflets

Handbills are an invaluable *aide-mémoire* but, if you are playing the big league, a well-planned leaflet will be a much stronger ally. Send leaflets rather than handbills to everyone on the mailing list.

A leaflet has the space to promote all those special features – a description of the play, of the location, the menu and an order form for the food. It must also carry a booking form and clear instructions as to how to obtain tickets.

Box office

The majority of your audience will come from your comprehensive mailing list and is unlikely to have direct access to a member of the cast. Make it easy. Offer as many ways as you can to get tickets. This is a time when a Freepost system, and a credit-card hotline can really pay off.

Timing

Timing can make or break an open-air show. This is not an event that most people will come to on the spur of the moment, it is a social occasion that must be planned for. Many of your audience will want to organize a party of friends. They may need to leave work early to take advantage of the opportunity of eating before the performance. If they are intending to bring a picnic, that too needs organizing.

Apart from the social side, open-air theatre is highly dependent on the weather. Those balmy evenings may turn out to be soaking wet. The British are amazingly optimistic when it comes to the weather, and you can sell the promise of summer sunshine in the spring. Try to sell the same promise a couple of months later in a wet June, and I don't fancy your chances.

If the tickets are booked and paid for, the weather is less of a problem; both the umbrellas and the audience will come out. From a mercenary point of view, if they don't, then at least you still have the cash.

Start early: the mailing list should swing into operation, at least three months before the appointed date. Even four months in advance is not too soon. Posters should be on the streets six to eight weeks ahead.

The press: the press are more difficult to control, but there too, your publicity must be much earlier than with a 'typical' play.

Make your first push into print, six months in advance, with information about the auditions, the casting, the proposed play, the director, etc. With an open-air production, this probably means January. The New Year may sound ridiculously early, but this is when people are beginning to plan their summer holidays and look forward to those sultry evenings that you are offering.

Get as many photographs into print as you can. Describing the delightful setting is all very well, but there is no substitute for actually seeing it. If your production has wonderful costumes, use them. A picture of an actor in jeans has half the impact of an actor in cloak and feathers.

Start to work the press about three months before, and aim for a big story a month after that. Your last major picture should be no later than three weeks before the show. If you can get more nearer the time, terrific, but, as we said before, very few people will come to this type of event on impulse. A picture the week of the show is too late to sell tickets.

Signposts

The location of an open-air event may well be off the beaten track and many of your audience will be unfamiliar with the area. Make it easy for them to find you and print a map on the back of the tickets and/or leaflets.

For an event which is likely to attract 500 or more cars, the Automobile Association (AA) will provide temporary signposts. Extra publicity for you, and a great help to the public.

Contact the AA at least eight weeks in advance by dialling Freephone number, 0800 393 808. After this initial contact, your request will be passed on to the appropriate regional office which will ring you back. There is a minimum charge of £100, which can increase depending on the number of signs.

7
Festivals

Festivals are a celebration of the performing arts. They offer an opportunity for the participants to demonstrate their skills to the public, and to learn from other groups in their field, whether it be music, dance or drama.

The complex task of designing a festival from scratch is the responsibility of the organizing committee as a whole and is outside the scope of this book. The following section therefore covers only those elements of the organization which the publicity team may find helpful.

A successful festival must establish an image and a reputation of quality that will ensure a steady supply of participants. This image will grow and develop over the years but must be constructed on a solid foundation of careful planning. A new festival, badly organized, may make a profit first time out but will crumble the following year because of loss of interest.

Festivals come in all shapes and sizes, but generally speaking they fall into two main categories, the competitive, and the non-competitive.

Competitive events

The first target of a publicity campaign must be the potential entrants. They not only dictate the final shape of the programme, but make a significant contribution to the financial success of the event – it is the participants who will sell the majority of the tickets. The initial contact with a potential entrant sets the tone of the event. Make it count.

Early-warning system

Both the organizers and the competitors want the same thing: a high standard of performance. Practice makes perfect, so allow for rehearsal time and notify everyone early. This can mean starting to plan the event as much as twelve months ahead. Once a festival is up and running, it is a simple matter to advertise next year's dates at this year's event.

The latest you can realistically start sending initial details out is six months in advance. This allows time for potential entrants to make up their minds, and for the organizing committee to finalize the programme.

As a general rule, the more people involved in an entry, the more notice they require. For example, to enter a full-length or one-act play, most groups will appreciate twelve months' notice. Societies often plan their productions a year in advance and have little flexibility, in either available membership or finance, to add a festival play to their list.

Schools also benefit from early information – they have timetables to plan.

Individual entries, on the other hand, will be happy to receive details nearer the time, say four to six months in advance. Indeed, tell them too early and they may forget all about it!

Entry hunting

A new festival needs to build a list of potential competitors. Head at once for your local library and raid any list that might possibly be of any use: local organizations, schools, colleges, arts associations, music teachers, youth groups, etc. Then either write to them, giving brief details of the new venture, or pick up the phone and start talking. One conversation will lead to another contact, and you should soon have a useful basic list.

An established festival will already have a comprehensive list of contacts but should also aim to have a subsidiary list of other individuals/groups who can be approached should the regulars be unable to appear.

These lists should be made available to the publicity team, so that posters, leaflets and order forms can be sent out nearer the time. Every individual taking part will want to bring their supporters. Make sure that this vast potential audience has little opportunity to escape.

Ticket Discounts

Friends of the competitors are already primed, and at least thinking about buying a ticket. Build on this and consider making them an offer they can't refuse – a cheaper ticket, even a free one.

Yes, of course, the festival needs all the money it can get but a drama festival in particular must have an audience. As we said before, playing to a handful of people after months of hard work is very disappointing. Competitors faced with a poor house may well decide that your event is not worth the effort and decline to come back another year.

There are many ways of running a discount system. Find one that is right for you. For example, for a team entry, offer one free ticket, or one free ticket for every ten sold, or 10-per-cent discount for bookings of ten or more. Similar offers can be made to a music or drama teacher who enters several pupils and so on.

At the very least, you should be prepared to allow all participants free access to the rest of the session that they have entered. They should not be expected to pay for the privilege of watching their rivals.

User-friendly festivals

A healthy festival, with a good reputation, will have competitors who come back year after year, bringing their audience with them. A satisfied competitor, who has enjoyed the experience and learnt something, even though he came twenty-ninth out of thirty entries, will come back. A competitor who has been pushed around, and who feels that the final awards were totally unfair, will not.

Tell them what they need to know. The rules and regulations must be crystal clear. Every entrant must have a copy in advance. Every entrant must know the time and place that they are expected to appear. Send them a map of the area, with the venue(s) clearly marked.

Tell them what facilities are on offer. Where do they park? Is there a piano? A play entry needs a vast amount of information. The last minute realization that a crucial piece of scenery is too big to go through the stage door can be disastrous.

Teams should be told ahead of time what lighting and sound equipment is available, and who will operate it. They need to know the size of the stage, how much room there is to manoeuvre the set, where the changing rooms are, and so on. Arrange for the groups to visit the hall and see for themselves.

On the day

A well-organized front of house is an important element in creating the festival image. Aim to create a sense of occasion, and to prevent chaos.

Competitors have worked long and hard for this day – don't spoil it for them. They are keyed up, nervous and, with their minds on their forthcoming performance, they need all the help they can get. Flustered competitors cannot give their best performance and will go away feeling cheated.

A busy event that involves several classes in different rooms of the same building, at the same time, can lead to confusion. Give every room a clear label, send the entrants a plan of the building, have spare plans available at the entrance and put up direction signs.

Provide human signposts, in the form of smartly dressed stewards. And give them a label too. Blank cardboard badges are easily obtainable and inexpensive.

The adjudicator

A competitive festival needs an adjudicator. He, or she, has a major impact on the success of the event. His name and reputation can attract entries and, by the same token, can put them off. Go for the best.

Learning from a festival is more important than the marks and certificates. The adjudicator must therefore have considerable expertise in his chosen field. He should be able to talk with authority but, most important, he should be able to pass on his knowledge to the competitors, clearly and constructively.

For music, dance and speech work, take the advice of the British Federation of Festivals. For drama, and the spoken word, you cannot do better than approach the Guild of Drama Adjudicators, GODA for short. GODA is the internationally recognized body for the adjudication of all forms of theatre. Founded in 1947, with membership limited to those with extensive experience of amateur and professional theatre, it is the longest established organization of its kind. (For addresses see Appendix: Useful addresses).

A good adjudicator is worth his weight in gold. Look after him. The following comments are based on GODA's notes for festival organizers, but are relevant to all adjudicators. Consider appointing a member of the organizing committee to act as the adjudicator's 'escort'. This member will then be responsible for ensuring the adjudicator has everything he needs during the performance.

The role of the escort could be extended to include travel and accommodation arrangements. Hotel accommodation should be close to the venue, but transport should be organized if necessary.

- Adjudicators need to eat, so make sure they have the opportunity for a meal.
- Before the performance, the adjudicators should be given sufficient time to inspect the stage, the lighting kit and so on, accompanied by the escort.
- Adjudicators need an uninterrupted view of the stage. Check beforehand where they prefer to sit.
- They need space to work. Ideally, they should be given a

73

table, with a shaded light which can be easily turned on and off.

- If a table is not possible, then a good-size clip-board is a reasonable substitute.

  Make sure that the clip-board has some means for securing papers, Adjudicators have enough to do without scrabbling about on the floor to find papers.

  Allocate a seat on either side of them to allow space for spreading papers, scripts and scores. In this situation, lighting can be a problem. A hand-held torch is not acceptable – you have engaged an adjudicator, not a juggler.

- Adjudicators need time to prepare scripts and set pieces. Send them complete scripts at least two weeks before the festival. A photocopy of an acting edition currently in print is unacceptable.

- Always provide a copy of the programme at each performance.

- Adjudicators need time to complete their notes at the end of each performance, and time to give verbal comments at the end of each section. Take this into account in the timetable of events and don't rush them.

Public publicity

So far we have an audience of participants and their friends and relations. There are other people out there who would be delighted to buy a ticket, so make sure they know!

Run the campaign with a standard package of posters, leaflets, and press coverage. The main problem with organizing a publicity drive for this type of festival is deadlines. You know what they are, but the participants have other concerns. Keep it simple and avoid having to rely on detailed input from the competitors themselves.

Posters and handbills

These need only carry the name of the festival, the place, the dates, the name of the adjudicator(s) and details of the box office. A basic background design can be used every year. This saves time, money, and creates a recognizable image of the event in the mind of the public.

Programmes

Programmes can be tricky. This time you really do need all the details from the competitors. Again, do not rely on their being as efficient as you are. Agree a deadline with the printer, then give the entrants a deadline that is two weeks earlier.

Press

Send a press release to all the local papers. Make sure that you get details into the arts page, and the 'What's on' listings. Offer free tickets to the arts correspondent; a review of the event is valuable publicity.

One problem with press coverage for competitive festivals is that photo opportunities are limited. Entrants only come together on the day, too late to help your ticket sales. A way round this is to encourage participating groups to arrange their own photo calls. This puts their society into the public eye, and the festival gets additional coverage.

A prize-giving ceremony is usually worth a picture. Although this year's festival is all over bar the shouting, it is a chance to consolidate its reputation, and to lay the foundations for next year. Even if no picture or review is available, send a complete list of the results and the prizewinners in time to make the papers the week after.

Non-competitive

These festivals are a showcase for the performing arts. They may focus on one specific area – dance, Shakespeare, music, etc. – or offer a whole variety of performances both professional and amateur. It is those festivals that offer a wide range of entertainment that present the publicity team with the greatest challenge. You must create a coherent image for the festival as a whole, while promoting each component event.

Publicizing this type of festival is a constant juggling act. The final balance between the whole and the parts, the number of posters that are distributed for one event rather than another, is never going to be perfect. You can only do your best, be aware of the issues involved and be prepared to learn from the experience of your particular festival.

Resist the temptation, to advertise everything, all at once, on every piece of paper you hand out. A poster that carries details of all the events on offer is crowded, virtually unreadable and therefore useless. Promoting the festival as a whole is obviously important, but to get the best from your publicity you also need to focus some of your resources on individual performances.

Give the festival a coherent image by choosing an aspect of design which can be used on all the publicity material: a graphic, a logo, even simply a colour.

Leaflets

Leaflets are the ideal vehicle to carry details of everything that is happening. An effective leaflet is a combination of press release, diary and booking form. That's a lot of information, so make it easy to read and keep the lay-out simple.

Avoid clutter: too many graphics and the reader will not see the wood for the forest of line drawings. Presenting the shows as a collection of mini-posters may seem an appealing idea, but makes it hard to extract the essential details of what, where, when and how much.

Headlines: good use of headlines helps to divide the leaflet into handy packets of information. Make the headline stand out by bold typeface and/or colour. A band of colour with white lettering is an elegant option.

The three methods of headlining that are most useful are dates, titles and category. Choose the one that suits you, and stick to the same system throughout the leaflet.

- *Dates*: it is a good idea to set your programme out in date order. When using a date as a headline, always include the day. Well, can you reliably say whether the 24th of next month is a Friday or a Sunday? Where there may be several events on the same day, it is helpful to include the time.

- *Titles*: if you decide to use the titles of the plays, or musical pieces as headlines, it is possible to vary the style of lettering to suit each item, but beware of over-complicating the page.

- *Category*: a few festivals may lend themselves to division into types of production, e.g. music, drama, workshops, etc.

Booking details: the most important part of the leaflet. For a festival dominated by professional groups and artists, you cannot rely on personal contacts to provide the audience. Make it as easy for the public to get tickets as you can.

Take time and trouble to design a postal-booking form that makes sense to the customer and to the box office. Freepost can be an invaluable asset for this type of promotion. Offer precise details of as many other methods of booking as you can, by credit card, telephone reservations, as well as by post. Check the information, then check again. A wrong or missing phone number will prove very expensive.

The parts

Posters and handbills have their part to play in advertising the whole festival but are best used to highlight particular items.

The question for the festival team is 'which items to highlight?' There are no hard and fast rules, you must go by instinct and experience. It is probably unwise to provide posters for every event, the public will be confused, and anyway you are unlikely to find enough different places to put them.

A poster can do two things for you:

- Promote a show that is selling well. A show with box-office appeal can pull in a new audience which may be converted into regular customers.

- Promote a show that is not selling. Festival publicity is a matter of balance – usually of bank balance, so consider giving special attention to an item where ticket sales are slow.

    For this technique to be most effective, you must be prepared to respond quickly. It helps to guess which are going to be the 'problem' shows well in advance, and to have artwork lined up and ready to go. It is also sensible to discuss the situation with your friendly neighbourhood printer and agree realistic deadlines.

Set a 'Judgement Day' to decide which posters to go with, and push the button.

The press
How do you decide the focus of a press campaign when you are trying to get over information about sixteen different shows? The answer is not to try. Leave it to the reporters and offer them a press conference. A press conference offers an opportunity for a reporter to get maximum information in the minimum space of time.

The conference team
Organize a 'panel of experts'. Invite artists, directors, organizers to be part of the team. They will be able to answer detailed questions in their own field and also offer an excellent opportunity for photographs.

The press pack
You have a mass of information to get across to the press, but don't expect them to absorb it in one go; they won't. Follow the tried and tested system of 'Tell them what you are going to tell them; tell them; then tell them what you have told them.'

Advance information
Prepare an information sheet and send it out at least two weeks ahead of the conference. Include:

1 Details of all the events in the festival.
2 Names of the artists attending the conference.
3 Names of festival personnel attending.

And don't forget to tell them the time and place of the conference itself!

Make a point of mentioning that there will be the opportunity to take pictures. Neither you nor the press will be pleased if they turn up without a camera. If you are certain that you will have a famous name in attendance, tell them that too. Be careful. If there is any doubt that the celebrity may not be able to come, always use phrases like 'we hope' or 'it is likely that'. Don't make a promise that you may be unable to keep – the press may not believe you next time.

Contact the key reporters the week of the conference and remind them.

Advance planning

Plan ahead. Don't rely on working it out as you go along. This ad lib approach is unprofessional, wastes time and usually means that some crucial piece of information gets lost in the chaos.

Write some form of agenda. Make notes of the key points that you want to communicate. Decide when and where photographs can be taken. Make sure that your 'panel' know what is expected of them, particularly if there is a possibility of a photograph. Leave time for the reporters to ask their own questions. If possible, arrange a room for individual interviews.

At the end of the meeting, send each reporter away with a press pack.

The press pack

A press pack is simply a collection of useful information – a handy reference guide. Include:

- A festival leaflet.
- More details on specific performances.
- Details of artists, and biographies.
- Details of visiting companies.
- Details of sponsors.
- Anything else you can think of.
- Your name and phone number for other queries.

8
Youth theatre

The basic techniques for publicizing a performance by a youth theatre are the same as for any other group. The difference lies in the style of the approach which should take into account the frequent changes in the membership, and the inexperience of the young people themselves.

There is a tendency to accept lower standards because of age, and this, together with the belief that the parents will come anyway, means that all too often publicity for these groups is last-minute and inadequate. Avoid this pitfall by taking a professional attitude, with the emphasis on training the young people and harnessing their energy.

In youth theatre, you have the perfect opportunity to train the publicity secretaries of the future, so, wherever possible, the job should be handled by a youngster. Train them well, and you never know, they could be after your job in a few years time.

The nature of a youth group, with an age range of 12–18 years, means there is little continuity. The members will need to take time out for examinations and school work. Interests can change, and some may leave the group altogether in favour of a new hobby. In an adult group the same person may hold a post for several years, and build up considerable expertise. Even when he resigns, he is usually still around to advise his successor. That cannot happen in a youth group. Continuity and advice must be built into the system some other way.

Designing the system

Be realistic, and aim for publicity secretaries of 15 or over. Give them the responsibility, but give them an adult back-up whom they can call on for advice.

Make sure that you define the respective roles.

Publicity secretary

The responsibilities of this role should include:

- Agreeing the budget.
- Planning the campaign.
- Writing letters.
- Booking boards, banners, etc.
- Collating material for posters, programmes, etc.
- Ensuring that all printer's deadlines are met.
- Organizing tickets.
- Liaison with box office.
- Press coverage.

Whilst the secretary *must* know exactly what is happening, it is sensible to form a sub-committee, not just of the secretary's mates, but across the ages. This ensures that other, younger members begin to learn the job, and that teamwork is encouraged.

The adult back-up

The back-up is ideally someone who has done the job and who could take over in the event of illness or impending disaster. He should be involved in the planning of the campaign and keep a watchful eye on the deadlines. But *no more*. His brief should be to resist the temptation to take an active role except when absolutely necessary.

Job description

The back-up can provide advice, but there is no substitute for a comprehensive job description. It is the key to ensuring an efficient publicity machine despite frequent changes in membership.

Maintaining the group's audience figures is important, but so is maintaining the enthusiasm of individual members. Nothing kills enthusiasm and initiative faster than panic. A well-thought-out, regularly updated document will save hours of precious time that would otherwise be spent scratching about for phone numbers and addresses. It will reduce the likelihood of missed deadlines and save the young publicity secretary many sleepless nights. A youth group changes fast enough without encouraging the resignations of desperate teenagers.

Keep it simple, but informative. The instruction 'Arrange posters' is certainly simple, but not a lot of use, so include:

- The address of the usual printer.
- The size and quantity usually ordered.

- The approximate cost.
- A list of suggested display sites.
- Recommended deadlines.

The words 'suggested' and 'usual' are deliberate. A job description is there to provide guidelines; it is not written in tablets of stone. Make provision for the document to be regularly up-dated. Encourage each publicity secretary to make notes as he or she goes along and arrange to have the revised version re-typed before the next person takes over.

Personal hand-overs are ideal, but not always possible in this type of group. The written information may be all the new publicity team will get.

Publicity matters

Youth groups are not famous for their fat bank accounts, and unfortunately the publicity budget is often the first to be cut. Be careful of false economy. Analysis of the accounts of the youth theatre that I am involved with, demonstrated that 85 per cent of our income comes directly from ticket sales, with 12 per cent coming from subscriptions, and 3 per cent from miscellaneous bits and pieces. Without successful ticket sales we would quickly run out of cash, and out of a group. It is therefore important to make the most of your limited resources and aim your publicity where it will have the most impact.

The target audience for a youth group can be divided into three sections, the three Ps: Parents, Peer group and Public. All three should be made aware of any production, but the balance of the campaign will change, depending on the type of show that is being promoted.

For a major production with family appeal, like *Annie* or *The Wind in the Willows*, you have a big potential audience, so pull out all the stops, press, posters, banners, go for as much publicity as you can get. On the other hand, a rehearsed reading or an evening of 'party pieces' is only going to appeal to people close to the performers. Save your money, cut back on the 'public' side – posters, leaflets, banners, etc. – and concentrate on the parents.

Parents

Parents form a significant proportion of your audience, but even they may not come if they don't know about it. Never assume that their children will tell them. Young people are notorious at forgetting the obvious. How many times have you discovered that there is a big school event the next day when you have already accepted another invitation?

Give parents the information well in advance, perhaps in a news-letter. Follow it up with a leaflet about a month before the show, and then, a couple of weeks later, with a ticket-order form. If you can afford it, at least one of these should be posted – pieces of paper given to young members have a peculiar habit of disappearing before they reach home. If not, then by making three attempts, you have increased the chances of getting something through!

Peer group

Peer group is used here not only to mean the best mates of group members, but anyone else of their age. You have a direct route to schools and colleges, so don't waste it! There is nothing like personal contact for selling tickets.

Encourage your members to take leaflets into their school, and to put up posters. Persuade them to approach teachers with an interest in the arts. Consider offering a favourable block-booking rate, specifi-cally for school parties.

Build up a list of local schools, including the name of the head teacher, or the head of the English department, and send details directly to them. The name is essential; in a busy school, a leaflet with no obvious pigeon-hole can end up as a mat for a coffee mug. And don't forget all those clubs – scouts and cubs, guides and brownies, football, ballet, and so on, and so on.

Keep a record of all the associations for future reference. In no time at all, you will have an invaluable mailing list.

Mailing list

A large proportion of your tickets will be sold through personal contact. Lose the contact and you lose the sale. A good mailing list can go a long way towards counteracting this problem. It offers the chance of maintaining some continuity in the face of a constantly changing membership, and of encouraging audience loyalty. It should include current members, schools, colleges, all the associ-ations mentioned above (and as many others as you can think of!) and should also carry details of past members.

The list needs to be regularly up-dated, at least once a year. There must be some system for dropping names that are no longer relevant. It is a waste of time and money to send letters to ex-members who have left the area, got married or now work in Australia. One method of ensuring reasonable accuracy is to make a small charge, enough to cover postage for the year, for every ex-member who wishes to be kept in touch with your activities.

Offer them the first year for free. The last newsletter of the year should carry a reminder that subscriptions to the mailing list are now due, how much it costs, and where to send the money. Thereafter, it is very simple, no subscription, no newsletter, and the name slides off the list. This system does not have to be restricted to ex-members. Anyone with an interest in the group can ask to be included.

Newsletters

Newsletters are an excellent means of communicating within a group, but are time-consuming and potentially expensive to produce.

Spread the work:

- Involve the whole membership in contributing. Of course, the newsletter should include details of forthcoming shows and events, but after that almost anything goes. You may have a budding poet, cartoonist, or someone who has a talent for devising crosswords. Why not use them?

- Appoint an editor from the membership. He or she should be responsible for gathering the material and for producing a draft copy.

- Appoint an adult back-up. Again, the back-up is there to provide advice and moral support, but also to check the draft before it is sent out. A youth-group newsletter should be fun, but it has a serious job to do, and an enthusiastic teenager may well miss out a crucial piece of information.

  The other role of the back-up, is as guardian of the group's image. What teenagers find hilarious, their parents may consider to be in very poor taste.

Control the cost:

- Agree the length of the newsletter. This may seem obvious, but that extra page doubles the amount of paper, and the printing/photocopying expenses will increase.

- Agree the number of issues and the timing. Aim to issue at least three a year. Ideally, to get full value from a newsletter as a publicity tool, aim to send one out about a month before each show. It is worth including a leaflet and/or ticket order form at the same time.

Group identity

A strong group identity can be very important to young people. Encourage the team spirit with group sweat shirts, T-shirts and badges. Ask their opinion first; group identity may be important, but this age range is very fashion conscious. Order a style or colour of sweat shirts that they would not be seen dead in and you could find yourself heavily out of pocket.

Badges with the group logo are fun, easy to wear and reasonably cheap. They can also be used to promote a specific show. Souvenir badges bearing the name of the show and a simple design are popular. Sell them to the cast before the show and they become portable advertising. Sell them to the audience as souvenirs, and with luck they will finally become profit.

Some companies will carry a stock of pre-designed badges for shows that are frequently performed, particularly pantomimes. A standard badge can cost as little as 20p and can realistically be sold for twice that amount. If you want to design your own badge, then the costs will increase depending on the artwork involved and the number of colours in the design. Check the economics before going ahead (see Appendix: Useful addresses).

Publicity mornings

Publicity mornings are the ideal time to wear all those sweat shirts and badges. Young people are far less easy to embarrass than their adult counterparts. They will relish the opportunity to walk down the High Street in full costume and make-up. And why not introduce street theatre? Discuss the idea of street theatre with the director. It does not need to be anything too grand, but any public performance needs planning and thinking about in advance. A short improvization based on the characters from the show is ideal.

Should your show involve interesting make-up, blood and scars, or animal designs, run a make-up demonstration, perhaps even offering to 'face paint' passing children. Always make sure that you have a willing 'victim', and the full permission of the parents.

Keep the team under control. Extrovert youngsters can go over the top. During any public appearance of this type, there should be a watchful adult in the background. At no time should any member of the public be made to feel uncomfortable or embarrassed.

Remember – youth theatre should be fun. It should not even begin to turn into yet another school project. Share the work, help them to plan, involve as many of the group as possible in the design and distribution of material, and *enjoy it*.

9
Over to you

Don't panic

Publicity is a major undertaking. Go slowly and never take on more than you can handle. Overloading yourself, or your group, is a recipe for disaster – deadlines will be missed, things will slip past by accident, mistakes will be made and the image of your group will suffer.

Tailor your publicity tactics to suit your group, not all of the ideas mentioned here will be appropriate or feasible for every company. Use this book as a guide, and do not hesitate to incorporate your own ideas. Whatever campaign style you choose, take it seriously and it will work for you.

Delegate

You do not have to do everything yourself!

Be organized

Make sure that everyone in the publicity team (including you!) knows precisely what is expected of them.

Make a note of names and phone numbers as soon as they are given to you and keep all relevant information in one place.

Deadlines, deadlines, deadlines

Know what the deadlines are and stick to them. The play will survive if an actor is ten minutes late for a rehearsal, but a programme which misses the printer's deadline will not.

So – there you have it. As I said at the beginning, theatre cannot exist without an audience. It is up to you to get those 'bums on seats'. Good luck and good fishing!

Appendix

Countdown

It is well worth taking the time to draw up a personalized plan of campaign. You have enough to do without having a last minute panic!

Plan ahead but do not place any firm orders until the play is cast and you are confident that it will actually happen. Deadlines and activities vary from group to group and are influenced by the nature of the performance and the extent of the audience that you wish to attract.

The following outline is for a typical show:

Week 12	Discuss poster/programme design. Approach advertisers/charities and sponsors. Arrange for promotional boards. Obtain permission for boards/banners, etc.
Weeks 11 & 10	Follow-up with advertisers. Agree poster/programme design. Follow up sponsors. Plan press campaign. Check deadlines.
Week 9	Discuss press campaign with producer and cast. Request details for programme from producer and cast. Poster design available. Approach celebrity guests.
Week 8	Send tickets, posters, handbills to printer. Arrange for photographs of cast (for programme and front of house
Week 7	Finalize press campaign. Arrange setting for press call.

	Contact the press with details. Organize distribution of posters/handbills.
Week 6	Programme to printers. Organize the sticking or sewing of the banner. Organize crew to erect banner.
Week 5	Contact press with 'taster'. Notify your group of publicity mornings. Notify your cast of proposed press call.
Week 4	Tickets available. Posters available. Handbills available. Contact press re main photo call.
Week 3	Poster/handbill distribution begins. Confirm details of press call.
Week 2	Banner goes up. Publicity morning. Press call.
Week 1	Programme available. Publicity morning.
SHOW TIME	Decorate foyer, etc. Relax!

Check pads

The publicity secretary has an enormous amount of information to handle, and a limited amount of time. The process will become second nature with experience, but for a newcomer the task can be daunting. The secret is in planning, organization and double checking.

It helps to devise a personal check list for each element of the campaign. Nothing looks quite so impossible if it is down in black and white.

Keep all the information in one place – when the phone rings with a problem at the other end, you need to put your hand on the relevant document in a hurry. Keep a quick reference guide next to the phone in the form of a check pad for each element of the campaign. That way you can record new information as it comes in, and avoid the problem of scraps of paper with vital details being scattered thinly across the house!

I have included some sample check pads, for posters, for the press and for programmes. Use them as a guide to develop your own.

POSTERS

PRODUCTION   Title ....

                      Dates ....

DESIGNER   Name ....

           Address ....

           ....

           Tel ....

PRINTER   Name ....

           Address ....

           ....

           Tel ....

QUANTITY   A4   A3

COST

DESIGN/ARTWORK TO
PRINTER BY   date ....

DELIVERY EXPECTED   date ....

NOTES

CHECK PAD 2

PRESS

LOCAL PAPERS

1 Name ....

Address ....

....

Tel ....

Contact ....

Copy day ....

Issue day ....

2 Name ....

Address ....

....

Tel ....

Contact ....

Copy day ....

Issue day ....

3 Name ....

Address ....

....

Tel ....

Contact ....

Copy day ....

Issue day ....

PHOTO CALL   Location ....

Contact ....

Tel ....

Date of call ....

(Celebrity guest) ....

Tel ....

CRITIC   Name ....

Tel ....

NOTES

PROGRAMMES

PRODUCTION	Title	
	Dates	
	Director Tel	
DESIGNER	Name	
	Address	
	....	
	Tel	
PRINTER	Name	
	Address	
	....	
	Tel	
PHOTOGRAPHER	Tel	
QUANTITY	COST	
ADVERTISING SPACE	No. of pages	
AD COSTS	Full page	£ ....
	Half page	£ ....
	Quarter	£ ....
	Back page	£ ....
COPY TO ME	Date	
COPY TO PRINTER	Date	
DELIVERY DATE	Date	
NOTES		

Useful addresses

This is a basic list of suppliers and contacts that I have found useful.

Printers

Cowdall's Printing Company
P.O. Box 1
16, Flag Lane,
Crewe
Cheshire CW1 3BQ
Tel: 0270 212389

Printing for the amateur theatre.
Handbills, posters, stickers, programmes and tickets.

Ticketshop
13, Cremyll Road,
Reading,
Berkshire RG1 8NQ
Tel: 0734 599234

Not just tickets (including computerized ticket numbering), but also handbills, posters and programmes.

Badges

Pantomime Presents
24 Victoria Street
Hessle
North Humberside
HU13 9NL
Tel: 0482 640497

The Guild of Drama Adjudicators

Honorary Secretary:
Mrs Jessica Eyre
8 Pound Crescent
Marlow
Bucks SL7 2BG
Tel: 0628 474718

The British Federation of Festivals

Festivals House
198 Park Lane
Macclesfield
Cheshire SK11 6UD
Tel: 0625 428297

Banners

Zephyr Flags & Banners,
Midland Road
Thrapston
Northants. NN14 4LX
Tel: 08012 4484

Banners with permanent lettering, flags, etc.

Performance Sails
Victoria Loft
Hillfurze
Bishampton,
Nr Pershore
Worcs. WR10 2NB
Tel: 0386 861161

Banners with removable lettering.

Index